WORDPOWER

WORD POWER

A TEST YOURSELF GUIDE

Second Edition

Neil Wenborn

KOGAN
PAGE

First published in Great Britain in 1981 by
Kogan Page Limited,
120 Pentonville Road,
London N1 9JN.
Second edition 1990.

British Library Cataloguing in Publication Data
A CIP catalogue record for this book is available from the British Library.

ISBN 0-7494-0054-4
ISBN 0-7494-0055-2 Pbk

Printed and bound in Great Britain by
Biddles Ltd, Guildford

Typeset by The Castlefield Press Ltd, Wellingborough Northants in
Baskerville 10.5/12 point.

Contents

Preface to the second edition

Even in the few years since the first edition of this book was published there have been many changes in the ways we use words. New usages have come and gone, trailing new abuses after them. Old abuses have strengthened their hold or finally let go. New words, too, have found their way into everyday English and old ones have departed. It is not so long since we would have stared blankly at someone who asked us to fax over the latest figures or told us that yuppies in the City were making a killing in junk bonds. We would have squirmed with discomfort at the thought of running a few projections through our laptops. And we would have taken offence if someone had called us green.

What has not changed, however, is the importance of wordpower itself. Never before has information travelled so fast or the ability to assimilate and react to it quickly and efficiently been so crucial in so many walks of life. To use that ability to the full, you must be able to make words work for you, whether you are writing a letter on the screen of your wordprocessor, reading a fax message, listening to a news report or presenting your company's latest product to a team of sales reps.

Language changes continually, but the purpose of language remains the same. In an age in which 'communications' have come to mean telephones and computer screens and public relations consultants, it is all too easy to overlook the fact that the basic tools of communication are still the words we speak and write. The best teleconferencing facility in the world will be mere plastic and circuitry if you cannot explain your ideas or understand what your opposite number is saying. And a PR consultant is only as good as his or her brief.

Terms and technology may change, but wordpower is as crucial today as it always was. Whether you are reading, listening, writing or speaking, the words you have at your disposal and the way you make them work for you are as important to successful communication now as they were when a sound bite meant having a good dentist and a spin doctor was a medic with a place in the local cricket team.

Introduction

COMMUTERS HIT BY CANCELLED TRAIN read a recent newspaper headline, no doubt from the same pen as the extraordinary pronouncement SMOKING INCREASES RISK OF DYING. Commuters who smoke would seem to stand little chance of survival these days, although it is surely encouraging to learn from the latter headline that death is not, as was previously thought, a 100 per cent certainty regardless of whether you smoke or not. Perhaps, indeed, this was the source of comfort hinted at by one well-respected television chat show host recently when he asked his guest, an equally well-respected politician, 'When you get really low, what is it that stops you going over the top?'

It is only too easy to overlook misuses of words, especially when you yourself are the guilty party. Because we generally know what we mean to say, we can easily assume that other people will understand us however sloppily or confusedly we express ourselves – and there can be few of us who have not at some time or other caught ourselves finishing a sentence with 'if you know what I mean' or 'if you get my drift'.

This book is all about making sure that people *do* know what you mean. Wordpower is not simply a matter of the number of words you know; it is also about the way you use those words, and the way you respond to other people's use of them.

If you have picked up this book and have read this far, you are no doubt already aware of some of the fascinations and frustrations of words. You no doubt already know how difficult (and how satisfying) it can be to find exactly the right word for the occasion, whether you are writing a letter to a friend or presenting a case at a committee meeting. This book is designed to make it a little easier to find that elusive word, and to help you to avoid some of the more common pitfalls of communication.

There are few areas of modern life in which words are not important, and few occasions when an ability to make them work for you is not a tremendous advantage. Careless talk may not often cost lives, but it can certainly cost time and money, especially in the business world where fast and accurate communication is essential and where the ability to put your ideas into words may be a crucial qualification. Whether you are filling in a job application form or trying to finish the crossword at lunchtime, wordpower is vital for success.

Wordpower: A test yourself guide looks at many of the more common uses and misuses of words, and includes a number of tests to help you to highlight some of your own strengths and weaknesses. These tests are meant to be fun to do, but they are also intended to be of practical use, and include, together with the kinds of puzzle that people have set themselves and their friends for centuries, examples of the types of test used by employers to assess the wordpower of potential employees.

This book may not turn you into another Dr Johnson or a celebrated after-dinner speaker, but it may at least help you to avoid the sort of verbal clanger which one housewife was reported recently to have dropped when, protesting her ignorance of a corpse the police had just found buried in her garden, she insisted that the body was 'a plant'.

Dead man's fingers, perhaps . . . ?

PART ONE:
WHAT IS WORDPOWER?

1. Why is wordpower important?

What your wordpower says about you

Words are the sounds we make in order to communicate with one another. These sounds are symbols of the things we think and feel. We also have symbols for these sounds, and it is these symbols you are looking at now. Because we have these symbols in common with other people who speak and read the same language as ourselves, we can communicate information and ideas not only to people we meet but also to people we have never met and never will meet. We can even communicate with people who have not yet been born, and can, without the paraphernalia of ouija boards and seances, receive information and ideas from people who died before we or our parents or our parents' parents were conceived.

With this extraordinary power – the power of words – at our disposal, it is hardly surprising that we should so often be judged by the way we use and abuse that power in our daily lives. This is more than ever true today when efficient exchange of information is crucial for the carrying on of effective business, and when the smallest breakdown of communication can lead to the loss of money, time and sometimes even lives. Obviously, you will be judged by what you do as well as by what you say, but the way in which you use words, both in speech and in writing, will inevitably be an important factor in people's overall assessment of you.

Language is also a powerful means of persuasion, and success in many areas of everyday life depends to a very large extent upon your ability to persuade people. You have to persuade an interviewer that you are the right person for the job. You have to persuade your bank manager to trust you with a loan. And if you are in a job that involves selling, you have to persuade potential buyers that your goods or the products of your organization are worth purchasing. Nor is it only in selling that an ability to persuade can be a major help on the career ladder. Many jobs involve a significant degree of persuasion, whether it is in managing your team to best advantage or in convincing your boss that you deserve a pay rise for doing so.

In everyday conversation, too, the ability to make your point concisely and clearly and to persuade the person to whom you are talking that your point is worth considering is an invaluable asset. There are few things more frustrating than not being understood, and the fault lies as often with the speaker as with the listener. Even a genuinely funny joke can be ruined if it is badly told.

Wordpower may not be the be-all and the end-all in determining your social and job success. It would count for little, for example, unless you also have a sympathetic understanding of other people's motives and reactions. But without it you will be at an immediate disadvantage. Given a straight choice between someone who speaks carelessly and writes in a woolly or muddled way and someone who presents his or her ideas cogently and attractively, most people, whether potential employers or potential clients, will obviously choose the latter. That person should be you.

Wordpower, then, is important not only in itself but also for what it implies about the sort of person you are. The massive strides forward that have been taken by the media in the course of the last 30 or 40 years have brought into people's living rooms models of presentation and communicational skills with which they cannot help but compare the people around them. Lazy or woolly speaking or writing, though still unsettlingly widespread, is probably more quickly spotted, and spotted by more people, today than ever before.

Woolliness in the use of words suggests woolly thinking, and woolly thinking is always inefficient. Words are a means of organizing experience and of marshalling ideas. The ability to use them efficiently will not only improve your own capacity for assimilating new ideas and for passing them on and making them work for you; it will also enable you to make that capacity known to other people. Administrative skills are based upon precisely such organizational abilities as these – and most jobs involve some degree of administration, if only in the planning of your personal workload. Employers often feel justified, therefore, in demanding a reasonably high level of wordpower in their employees and in candidates applying to them for certain jobs.

Wordpower is also about the way you respond to other people's use of words. We live in an age of almost instantaneous communications. From the dealing rooms of the great financial institutions to the fax machines churning away in thousands of offices throughout the world, information travels faster today than ever before. As a result it is more than ever essential to bring a clear and perceptive mind to what you read, hear, write or say. You must be able to pick out of a document or report quickly and accurately those elements which are most important to the argument being put forward or to the particular situation in which you find yourself. You must also be able to react speedily and appropriately to verbal directives.

Accuracy, not impressiveness, is the hallmark of effective communication. Indeed, for speech or writing to be *genuinely* impressive it must, whatever else it may do, convey the speaker's or writer's meaning as accurately as possible. Mere superficial impressiveness suggests a lack of substance in what is actually being said, and will probably not survive the closer scrutiny to which it will almost certainly be subjected. In speech such use of language will sound like bluff or bluster. In writing it is apt to lapse into jargon (see page 35) or verbosity.

Unfortunately, there are only too many examples of this type of writing. A brief quotation from one such example may serve as a salutary warning, the more so since the subject of the extract is the way people talk to one another:

> In natural conversation, therefore, members must ongoingly
> monitor utterances for possible turn-transition-relevant
> points; similarly, with the items which come to fill what will
> be preceding turns or slots, members must ongoingly both
> search for the methodic basis of their selection and locate the
> prospective consequentiality of such selections for future talk.

So now you know.

The practical importance of wordpower

One of the things Confucius really *did* say is: 'If language is not correct, then what is said is not what is meant; if what is said is not what is meant, then what ought to be done remains undone.'

This statement is a fine example of practising what you preach: it is difficult to imagine a more precise exposition of the importance of accurate communication, and Confucius' words are as true today as they were when they were written, more than two thousand years ago. Efficient use of language is vital for efficient action. The inexperienced pilot who has to be 'talked down' by ground control has become something of a cliché in disaster movies, but it is not only in such dramatic circumstances as these that every word counts towards success or failure. Marketing people know that the wording of a mailing shot will make a tremendous difference to the response it elicits. A letter beginning 'Dear Sir or Madam, We wish to bring to your attention . . . ' is unlikely to get a second glance from people weaned on the punchiness of newspaper headlines and the eye-catching slogans of billboard advertising. Again, a poorly constructed letter, inaccurately summarizing the substance of a business meeting, can lose a potential client or create false and potentially costly expectations. In the ever more competitive world of modern business, misuse of words can be a very expensive failing.

Similarly, official forms have to be carefully worded so that people filling them in will know what information is required of them. In their instructions, the compilers of such forms have to narrow the range of possible answers to each question so that the one they receive is the one they want. Some, unfortunately, have still not realized that unnecessary wordiness, long sentences and complicated constructions are the surest way to confuse the recipient and to give themselves the extra work of sorting through haystacks of irrelevant information to find the factual needle they really want. As with any other form of communication, the key to success is imagining yourself in the reader's (or listener's) place. Always ask yourself what information is required and speak or write accordingly.

Nor is it only in professional life that your use of words can have an immediate practical effect. It is equally true in everyday conversation. For example, the way you answer when people ask you directions to somewhere will decide whether or not they get there. There is a lesson to be learned here too: if you stop and think before replying, you are far more likely to give exact, helpful and easily followed directions than if you leap straight in and then have to change your instructions halfway through.

The same applies to almost anything you have to say or write. If you are sure in advance of what you want to put across, you will be far more likely to convey your meaning accurately. And you cannot disguise the effects of woolly thinking. The radio interviewer who asked his guest 'Was there much respect that you had for your boss?' broadcast to everyone that he had not thought out in advance the question that he wanted to ask. 'Did you have much respect for your boss?' is clear and straightforward and would have taken a couple of seconds' more thought to phrase.

There is a party game in which one person whispers a short message to a second person and the second person passes on what he or she has heard to a third person, and so on. By the time the message reaches the final player it is often virtually unrecognizable to the person who began the game. The same sort of thing can happen in everyday communication. Muddled thinking results in inaccurate statements, inaccurate statements result in misleading information, and misleading information is passed from person to person until the errors reveal themselves in action, often with disastrous consequences.

Sir Winston Churchill lamented the fact that most of the things we have to read in the course of our daily work are far too long, and that much valuable time and energy is wasted in looking for the essential points. Such wordiness is often the result of muddled thinking, of people only working out what to say once they have started saying something else. A little careful forethought would halve the size of a good many pieces of writing and would save a lot of people a lot of unnecessary reading and puzzling and annoyance.

The things we say and the things we do are intimately connected. And the words we use say something about our history. For example, the fact that such terms as privatization, silicon chip, AIDS and the greenhouse effect are now widely used and understood reflects the course of recent events and discoveries. So now let us look at the relationship between wordpower and vocabulary – the relationship between the way we use words and the words we know.

Wordpower and vocabulary

Wordpower, as we have seen, is about very much more than the number of words you know. But at the same time words are the raw material of communication and the greater your vocabulary is the greater will be the means at your disposal for efficient communication.

It has been estimated that an average adult vocabulary is about 18,000 words, but it is difficult to know quite what this figure means. For example, does it include that verbal no-man's-land of words whose meanings you think you know when you see them used in a specific context but which you would find difficult to define if asked to do so? (Many words, including perhaps a few of your own *bêtes noires*, appear in the definition tests towards the end of the book – see pages 59–93.)

Perhaps a more meaningful figure would be the number of words a person regularly uses in his or her everyday life. Someone may *know* a large number of words but only *use* a very small percentage of those words. The number of words used will, in fact, depend upon that person's word*power*. And yet, even this sort of figure (were it calculable) would be of limited use. There are, for example, certain

17

primitive languages which have a large number of words representing various different kinds of, say, cutting, but which have no word for 'cutting' itself. What are we to say of the 'wordpower' of someone who has a broad vocabulary in a language such as this?

Leaving these speculations aside, though, it is self-evident that having a wide vocabulary will give you a correspondingly wide choice of words for what you want to say. This does not mean that in any given situation you will have a choice of various different ways of saying what you want to say, all of which will equally convey your meaning; this would hardly be an advantage. It means, rather, that in certain situations a wide choice of vocabulary will enable you more exactly to pin down and convey to a listener or reader the meaning you intend to convey.

This in itself may not seem to be an unqualified boon. It is, of course, true that the more words you have to choose from, the more difficult it will be to make the choice. But it is also true that a wider choice means a better chance of finding the *right* word. And anyway, no one ever claimed that accurate communication was easy.

Choosing the right word can be a painful business, but the satisfaction of finding it (and you almost always know when you *have* found it) is generally worth all the effort. It is always easier to choose the first word that comes to mind than to struggle for the most precise one you can find, but first words, like first impressions, are not always accurate. It is easier to say that a plan is 'good' than to ask yourself what you mean by good and then say that instead. St Francis and blancmange could both be called good, but not, one assumes, in the same way as your plan. Blanket words cover up proper distinctions; they do not cover up lack of thought. And laziness is woven large in the fabric of most of them.

At the same time, no one with the interests of accurate communication genuinely at heart would dream of saying 'pulchritude' for 'beauty', 'nigritude' for 'blackness' or 'osculate' for 'kiss'. The dangers of verbosity are almost as great as the dangers of laziness. Either way you will not be making your meaning as clear as possible.

The novelist Arnold Bennett used to put aside a certain length of time each day for reading the dictionary. Arthur Scargill has said that his father used to do the same. Dictionaries are certainly fascinating things and can lead you on interesting word chases from cross reference to cross reference, but they are of limited use for the purpose of extending your vocabulary. This is partly because the definitions they give for words appear in a sort of verbal limbo, whereas the process of speaking or writing is precisely the process of putting words in contexts. The dictionary, for example, will tell you that *capillary* means 'of hair', but saying that you have just been to the barber's and had a capillary cut will not do much for your barber's reputation. There is really no substitute for reading as a means of extending your vocabulary. It is only by reading, and reading with care, that you can be sure of widening your knowledge of words and how to use them. Dictionaries are invaluable for looking up the meaning of words you find in context but they do not tell you how to use words yourself.

Spelling

What about the way you represent words on paper? Is spelling important?

One cannot help being irritated sometimes by the illogical nature of English spelling. There can be few children who have not at some stage asked why, if 'tough' is pronounced 'tuff', 'bough' is not pronounced 'buff' and 'through' is not pronounced 'thruff', or vice versa. As a result of these illogicalities many people have made attempts to reform and standardize the spellings of English words. But, in the words of Walter Ripman and William Archer in their book *New Spelling,*

> think ov dhe meny wurdz dhat wood have to be chaenjd if eny real impruuvment were to rezult. At dhe furst glaans a pasej in eny reformd speling looks 'kweer' and 'ugly'. Dhis objekshon iz aulwaez dhe furst to be made; it iz purfektly natueral; it iz dhe hardest to remuuv. Indeed, its efekt iz not weekend until dhe nue speling iz noe longger nue, until it haz been seen ofen enuf to be familyar.

This passage proves its own point. Laudable though the aims of standardization may be, there is no change made in the above paragraph that can be said to advance the cause of communication. Reformed spelling of this kind also makes implicit assumptions about pronunciation. In the passage just quoted, for example, the authors have evidently decided that 'often' is to be pronounced without the 't' being sounded. The administrative problems involved in introducing a system of spelling such as this are obviously too great for it to be more than an ideal (if indeed it is even that), and there is surely still less of a case for teaching children 'phonetic spelling' as an introduction to 'accepted spelling', since this involves learning one system, and then unlearning that system and learning another one.

But to return to the opening question: is spelling important? The simple answer is Yes. With all its absurdities and logical inconsistencies, 'accepted spelling' remains the way in which the vast majority of people represent the sounds we make when we are speaking, and any deviations from that accepted norm serve only to distract the reader. Worse still, they inevitably suggest carelessness, and with some justification. If, for example, an employer is presented with an application for a clerical job which is full of incorrect and inconsistent spellings, he or she will have good reason for thinking that the applicant concerned is also unmethodical in his or her approach to other matters. Nor will the employer want to hire someone whose letters and paperwork would reflect that inconsistency on to the company itself.

Of course, we all have our blind spots where spelling is concerned – words we have to look up in the dictionary every time we want to use them – and in a language as full of exceptions as English, few people indeed will be perfect spellers. But frequent mistakes and inconsistencies *do* matter, not only in themselves but also, like every other aspect of the way we use language, for what they suggest about the sort of people we are.

2. Uses and misuses of words

Misuses of words

Language is continually changing, and the way in which each of us uses words in his or her daily life influences, to a greater or lesser extent, the direction of that change. Many words and expressions which were considered awkward or unusual only a hundred years ago are common currency today, while others which would have seemed quite natural and proper to our great-grandparents have now become archaic or have dropped out of use completely.

For example, when, in 1780, Jeremy Bentham wrote his influential book *Introduction to Principles of Morals and Legislation,* he felt called upon to apologize for his use of a newly coined word, *international,* which is now to be found in every daily newspaper produced in the English language. In his apology, however, he excused his use of the word on the grounds that it was 'sufficiently analogous and intelligible'. Although we now refer to 'analogue computers' and still use the word 'analogous' to mean 'similar' or 'parallel', it is many years since it carried Bentham's meaning of 'having models or parallels'.

Again, very much more recently, Hunter Diack published a book on wordpower in which he wrote of his difficulty in finding the meaning of an obscure New Zealand term, *hang gliding.* His book was first published in Great Britain in 1975, since when changes in sporting fashion have made hang gliding something of a household word. Similarly, the 1976 *Concise Oxford Dictionary* lists some 17 meanings of the word *green,* but not one of them refers to the environmental context in which it now appears daily in our newspapers.

If, then, so much of the way in which we use language is a matter of changing fashions and idioms in speech and writing, what actually constitutes 'misuse' of words? We have already looked at some of the uses of language and at the importance of wordpower, and have seen the ever-increasing need for accurate communication. In the broadest sense, words are 'misused' whenever they militate against that accuracy. Just as a sculptor uses a chisel to 'release the figure from the stone', so, when you are speaking or writing, you are using words as the tools with which to chisel out your meaning. And that meaning will suffer or become distorted if you use the wrong tools at the wrong times or if (to push the simile as far as it will go) you use tools which are already blunt from overuse.

A book many times the length of this one would be required if one were to attempt a comprehensive listing of the misuses to which the English language is subject, and anyway there are a number of excellent books already on the market which go a long way towards doing precisely that. All there is time for here is a brief look at some of the more common verbal pitfalls. Many of the tests later on in the book are also designed to keep you on your toes, linguistically speaking, and include specific examples from some of the areas considered in general terms in the following pages.

The right word for the job

It is ironic that one of the most abused words in the English language – the word *nice* – originally meant 'precise', a meaning it retains in the well-worn phrase 'a nice distinction'. More about 'nice', and other words like it, appears in the section on overused words (see page 29), but for the time being this unfortunate little adjective may serve nicely to introduce that central tenet of wordpower – precision in choosing your words.

Certain lax usages have become rife in recent years and have been known to infect even the most careful speakers. From everyday speech these usages have now, more worryingly, found their way into written English. Perhaps the chief among these abuses is the use of the word *hopefully* to mean 'it is to be hoped'. 'Hopefully, I shall be arriving on the first train from town' means, if it means anything at all, 'I shall be arriving full of hope on the first train from town'. It does not mean 'I hope to be arriving on the first train from town'. Again, 'The average wage and, hopefully, the standard of living should begin to rise by the end of the year' is grammatically a nonsense, since a standard of living cannot be hopeful any more than it can be neurotic or drunk. The word *thankfully* has begun to suffer from the same misapplication in phrases like 'Thankfully, I escaped before the car blew up' (which is no doubt true, but not exactly what the speaker meant), 'Thankfully, I wasn't there when the car blew up' (which cannot be given the benefit of the doubt) and 'The car, thankfully, didn't blow up' (which, even allowing for the fact that people invest their cars with human attributes like bloody-mindedness, means nothing at all). In each phrase the word thankfully could be replaced by 'fortunately' without any loss to the intended meaning.

Hopefully and thankfully are misused partly out of laziness (though it is surely a misplaced sense of convenience that prefers hopefully to 'I hope') and partly because people like to avoid tags beginning with 'I' when they are either trying to sound impressive or trying to dodge the issue. The politician who says 'The rate of inflation will, hopefully, decrease over the next few months' is probably chiefly hopeful that he will not be personally called to account if the inflation rate suddenly soars by 20 per cent. Similarly, if your boss asks you when you will submit a certain report and you reply 'Hopefully, it will be ready by Wednesday', you will, by leaving yourself out of the picture, sound as if you are trying to make the report itself responsible for its own appearance or failure to appear on the specified date!

Another word which is frequently used in the wrong sense is *momentarily*. Momentarily means 'for a moment'. It does not mean 'in a moment' or 'very soon'. Thus, 'The plane will be landing momentarily' means not that it will be here any minute but that it will touch down and take off again within the space of a few seconds.

Aggravate is another word which has come in for more than its fair share of insensitive handling. 'To aggravate' properly means 'to intensify', particularly in the sense of making worse, but it is used far too often to mean 'to annoy'. You can aggravate a patient's pneumonia by putting him or her in a cold room, but you should not be able, by your thoughtless action in so doing, to aggravate that patient's solicitous friends and relations. To object to this colloquial use of the word aggravate to mean 'annoy' or 'exasperate' is perhaps to fight a losing battle when even so redoubtable a wordsmith as Charles Dickens uses it in this sense. But it does nonetheless seem a pity that its useful original meaning should be swallowed up, when we already have a number of other words which will satisfactorily do the job of meaning 'to annoy'.

A more recent recruit to the ranks of the great misused is the word *optimistic*. Optimism originally meant the philosophical doctrine that everything is for the best in this, the best of all possible worlds. Now it means a predisposition to look on the bright side of things. It is a state of mind, not a reaction to a particular set of circumstances. All those politicians, businesspeople and commentators who, when interviewed about the outcome of negotiations, say they are 'optimistic' may well habitually believe that evil will eventually

23

triumph over good in the world, but that is not normally what they are being asked about. What they mean is that they are 'hopeful' that the negotiations will succeed (not, of course, that the negotiations will hopefully succeed!).

There are also a number of pairs of words whose meanings are regularly confused. *Alternate* and *alternative* is one such pair. 'Alternate' means 'by turns', as in the sentence 'High Street and College Road are served by alternate buses' (ie, the first bus goes to High Street, the second to College Road, the third to High Street, the fourth to College Road, etc). 'Alternative' means 'available as one of two choices'. Thus, 'If you don't want to go to College Road, you can catch the alternative bus to High Street'. 'Alternative' can also be used as a noun, of course, as in 'The alternative to the High Street bus is the bus to College Road'. (You cannot have more than two alternatives. After that, what you have are options.)

Disinterested and *uninterested* have long suffered a similar identity crisis. Disinterested means 'unbiased' and uninterested means 'not interested'. You can show a disinterested concern for someone's welfare, but you cannot show an uninterested concern for anything.

At least these pairs of words have basic meanings in common. Others are misused without even that excuse. Take *mitigate* and *militate*. To mitigate (which comes from the Latin word for 'mild') means 'to alleviate' or 'to reduce the severity of'. To militate (which comes from the Latin word for 'soldier') means 'to have force', especially where one set of facts has greater force than ('militates against') another. Thus, in a criminal case, the evidence may militate against the conclusion that an offender is responsible for his or her actions. As a result his or her sentence may be mitigated. But no evidence can 'mitigate against' any other evidence.

Similarly, *composed* and *comprised*. A given whole can be composed of its parts or it can comprise its parts. It cannot, despite the attempts of numerous journalists and broadcasters, 'comprise of' or 'be comprised of' its parts.

More surprising still is the confusion between *bought* and *brought* which seems to have crept into the broadcast media. It cannot be said too often that bought is the past tense of buy and brought is the past tense of bring. They are not, and never have been, interchangeable.

You can test your knowledge of 50 pairs of words whose meanings are often confused in the test on page 76.

Many other examples of loose or incorrect usage could be enumerated, but the point is clear. Always work out precisely what you want to say, and choose your words as carefully as the time

24

available allows. Do not simply use the first word that comes to mind unless it is the word that most accurately expresses your meaning. Never try to say things in a more complicated way than is necessary, but, at the same time, do not shy away from the unusual word if it conveys your meaning more nearly than the generally accepted word. Contexts are treacherous things, and once they have got hold of a word they tend not to let it go until it has lost all its strength. Always assume, as is indeed often the case, that you are going to be questioned closely about what you say or write. Do not, for example, say something is 'relatively unimportant' unless you have an answer ready for the interviewer who asks 'relative to what?' Again, ask yourself whether you really need to use tags such as 'in the context of', 'with respect to' or 'in terms of' and, when you are writing, be wary of using inverted commas to suggest that a word is not quite the right one for the job, but is close enough. If it is the wrong word, it is worth taking time to find the right one, and if it is genuinely as close as you can get to what you mean, let it stand without implied apology. Above all, remember that woolly writing suggests woolly thinking, and that woolly thinking is always inefficient.

Grammatical mistakes

Grammar is the science of the mechanics of language, and is therefore about the precise way in which we put our thoughts into words. Many people think of grammar, if they think of grammar at all, as a sort of unenlightened despot, imposing rules from above without regard to the needs or convenience of its struggling subjects. It is easy to forget that language came before grammar, and that grammar is merely an attempt to systematize the way we use words, in order to avoid misunderstandings and ambiguities.

It would be futile to attempt to list here even the rudiments of grammar, but it is worth repeating the general point that the purpose of language is first and foremost to communicate. Anything which serves to obstruct that purpose, whether or not it is in accordance with the rules of grammar, constitutes a misuse of words. For example, there is nothing grammatically wrong with the following sentence: 'Here is the mouse the cat the dog killed caught'. However, no one who wanted to make his or her meaning clear would seriously consider using this form of words.

Similarly, only a pedant would think of saying 'this is something up with which I will not put', although again there is nothing grammatically incorrect about it. Most of us were taught at school

25

that it is 'wrong' to end a sentence with a preposition (*by, with, from,* etc) but, as the above example shows, there are times when not to do so would result in the most ridiculous expressions.

On the whole, though, the rules of grammar are there to make life easier and are worth observing. They have been carefully formulated to reduce to a minimum the opportunities for confusion and ambiguity which language presents at every turn. Take, for example, the construction '*both . . . and . . .* '. There is a rule that no part of speech coming between the 'both' and the 'and' can be taken as read after the 'and', but must be repeated if necessary. Thus, in any sentence containing a 'both . . . and . . . ' clause, it should be possible to remove all the words from 'both' to 'and' inclusive and still be left with a sentence that makes sense. For example, look at the sentence:

A good conversationist must be able both to speak well and listen well.

If you take out all the words from 'both' to 'and' inclusive, you are left with 'A good conversationist must be able listen well', which makes no sense. Since the 'to' comes between the 'both' and the 'and' it cannot be taken as read after the 'and'. One way of setting the sentence to rights, then, would be to put the 'to' before the 'both':

A good conversationist must be able to both speak well and listen well.

Another way would be to leave the 'to' between the 'both' and the 'and' but to repeat it after the 'and':

A good conversationist must be able both to speak well and to listen well.

Other versions of the sentence are also possible:

A good conversationist must both be able to speak well and be able to listen well.

A good conversationist must be both able to speak well and able to listen well.

All the above variants are grammatically acceptable, and is up to the individual speaker or writer to decide which one he or she finds most appropriate or pleasing to the ear.

This may seem a pedantic rule, since the meaning of the sentence concerned is anyway quite clear. There will be cases, however, where the rule can be used to help clarify the meaning. For example, look at the sentence 'In times of distress, children must be able to turn to both their parents and their playmates for comfort'. The statement as it stands is ambiguous. It could even be construed as an indirect attack on one-parent families. If the sentence is recycled to read 'In times of distress, children must be able to turn both to their parents and to their playmates for comfort' any such interpretation is precluded. A grammatical rule has enabled us to make our intention clear. (The same rule applies, of course, 'to *either . . . or . . .*', '*neither . . . nor . . .*' and '*not only . . . but also . . .*'.)

English is an eccentric language and just as there are exceptions to its rules of spelling and pronunciation so there are exceptions to its grammatical rules. One example will show how these exceptions can come about and become accepted simply as a result of the way in which ordinary people use words in their everyday lives.

There is a very solid and sensible rule of grammar which states that plural subjects should not be attached to singular verbs (ie, that we should not say 'The reasons for this is as follows' or 'Jane and her friend Elizabeth is walking down the road'). This may seem self-evident (although it is surprising how often, especially in long sentences, you find that people get it wrong) but when did you last hear a television announcer say 'Those were the news; now for the weather'? Such a construction would sound absurd to us now, but the only authority for not using it is the fact that the majority of people have decided to speak of the news in the singular.

On the same subject, what do you do with borderline cases such as *graffiti* and *data,* both of which are plural nouns? You will no doubt have seen these words attached to both plural and singular verbs, and there are indeed two schools of thought as to whether or not 'data is . . . ' and 'graffiti is . . . ' are unacceptable. More people might frown on you for using *the media* with a singular verb (though it happens often enough, even among the media's own personnel). But then again how many times have you heard the little wooden cube in packaged board games referred to as *the dice* without anybody rushing for the dictionary to prove that 'dice' is the plural of 'die'?

The way in which you use these words will affect the way in which future generations use them, and will help to determine the point at which, in this direction at least, what 'sounds right' takes over from what is 'grammatically correct'.

Colloquialisms

Colloquialisms are simply words and phrases which are found in familiar speech. Everyone, to a greater or lesser extent, speaks differently from the way in which he or she writes. But, as we have already seen, the way in which people speak to one another has a powerful influence upon the way the language is written down, and therefore upon the way it is passed on to the reading public of the next generation.

What, then, you may wonder, is a section on colloquialisms doing under the general heading 'Misuses of words'? There is, obviously, nothing 'wrong' with colloquialisms. Indeed, there is a closer relationship today between spoken English and what used to be called 'formal English' (ie, the sort of English that is used on formal occasions) than has ever existed before, a fact which is almost entirely attributable to the unprecedentedly wide availability of radio and television. You have only to look at a 'standard' business letter to see how much more colloquial are the uses of today than those of, say, 30 years ago. Further, some very useful words and phrases have come into the language through the medium of colloquial usage. Few people would now object to the use of words such as *brunch* (meaning a combination of breakfast and lunch in a single meal), *squirearchy* (the class of landed proprietors), *guesstimate* (that ever-useful word meaning an estimate based on a combination of guesswork and reasoning) and *laser* (a popular acronym for *l*ight *a*mplification by *s*timulated *e*mission of *r*adiation). Nor would *breathalyser* (breath analyser) or *transistor* (transfer resistor) cause many eyebrows to be raised. And, recent coinage though it is, it would be difficult to think of an equally concise synonym for the ubiquitous *yuppie*.

Again, colloquial usage has helped to give new meanings to words, or to develop sides of their meaning which were previously neglected. This is the case, for example, with the word *liaison* (and the more recent back formation *liaise*) which is listed in the 1976 edition of the *Concise Oxford Dictionary* only in its sexual and military senses but which has now come to be used far more widely to mean a close working relationship.

But the overspill of colloquialisms into written English has also led to some unfortunate misuses, many of which have now become established. The words *hopefully, thankfully, momentarily, aggravate* and *optimistic* have already been considered (see page 22). Other examples of words whose proper meaning has been changed or weakened by colloquial usage include *awful* (which originally meant 'awe-inspiring'), *dreadful* (which can now be applied to anything from the price of eggs to the prospect of nuclear war), *chronic* (which technically means 'lingering' or 'permanent', particularly in relation to disease, but is now often used simply as a synonym for 'bad') and *terrific* (which properly means 'causing terror', but has come, by a very roundabout route, to mean 'excellent', as in 'it was a terrific party'). All these colloquialisms have weakened the power of the words concerned and can therefore be regarded as misuses.

The problem of when to use words and phrases that are normally confined to popular speech is largely one of judging what a particular occasion demands. For example, a potential employer might well be expected to flinch if, when he or she asked you about your interests at an interview, you replied that you were 'heavily into rap'. Again, you would be unlikely to endear yourself to your bank manager if you ended your letters to him or her with 'Cheers for now' or 'See you', whereas close friends would be justified in wondering what had come over you if you signed your Christmas cards 'Yours faithfully'.

Perhaps a useful distinction to bear in mind is that between colloquialisms and slang. Although the dictionary is not necessarily the ultimate arbiter in these matters, you might find it interesting to look up a few of the words and phrases that you use quite frequently and see whether the dictionary classes them as slang or as colloquialisms. For example, the *Concise Oxford Dictionary* regards 'sack' as slang when used in the sense of 'bed', but as a colloquialism when used in the sense of 'dismiss from service'. This distinction reflects the way the word is used in everyday life. It would not be inappropriate, even in a fairly formal speech, to refer to having given someone the sack; eyebrows might well be raised, though, if you ended the speech by announcing that you were off to hit the sack. On the whole, then, it is safest to steer clear of slang on more formal occasions unless you have a very good reason for using it.

A similar long-standing problem is when to use contractions such as *don't, didn't, won't, haven't,* etc. With words like these, as with so many other colloquialisms, 'misuse' is largely a matter of context. The 'don't' and 'didn't' family is still considered out of place in certain kinds of writing, but at other times 'do not' and 'did not' can sound pompous and absurd. Again, it is really up to you to decide where the dividing line should be drawn.

Overused words

We have already mentioned the fate of that long-suffering little word 'nice'. It is a fate which has overtaken many of its relatives too, words whose integrity has been eroded by too much contact with unsuitable companions.

Many of the words most notoriously overused today are superlatives. The entertainments business, in particular, is a great promoter of these. How many times have you heard 'my next guest' described as 'the lovely . . . ', 'the very lovely . . . ' or even 'the very very lovely . . . '? Words like *marvellous, wonderful* and *superb* are hardly given a second glance these days unless they are accompanied at the very least by a *very* and preferably by an *absolutely,* an *indescribably* or an *incredibly. Adorable* and *divine* have long since been robbed of their religious connotations in the general rush to unearth still more exalted adjectives to set this breakfast cereal apart from all other breakfast cereals, or to paint that package holiday to the Costa del Sol as the package holiday to end all package holidays.

Many fields of vocabulary have been invaded by the forces of overuse. Psychology has lost *traumatic* to the enemy; biology has yielded *viable.* A difficult shopping trip can now be described as 'traumatic' even though the likelihood of it having genuinely constituted a severe emotional shock is surely very small. And none of the many suggestions and proposals, the myriad plans and policies, to which the term 'viable' is applied can with any truth be said to be 'capable of organic growth'.

Again, what would Jane Austen have thought of the way every mail-order catalogue or holiday-camp brochure is now described as *literature* or even as '*the* literature'? What would the signatories of the American Declaration of Independence have felt about the way every letter, memo or even computer file has now turned, as if by magic, into a *document*?

Why, in our broadcasts and newspaper reports, has every danger suddenly become a *real* danger, or, worse still, a danger *in a very real sense?* What constitutes an unreal danger?

Look, too, at the way the word *approximately,* a long-standing favourite with those who are trying to hedge their bets, has come to mean quite the opposite of itself in certain contexts because of the way we habitually overuse superlatives. 'Approximately', now used simply as a synonym for 'roughly', really means 'very nearly'. Therefore, when people speak of a statistic as 'very approximately x', they are not saying (as they almost always think they are) that x is a very rough estimate of that statistic; they are saying precisely (or imprecisely) the opposite – that x is a very accurate estimate.

Another word whose meaning has almost become reversed by overuse is *discrimination*. It is not many years since a person who was credited with 'discrimination' might well have felt pleased with himself or herself. Who, indeed, could possibly object to being thought possessed of sufficient judgement and taste to be able to choose disinterestedly (see page 24) between the options available? However, with the development of interest in such important issues as women's rights and the welfare of minority groups, the word has suffered an unfortunate shift of meaning, and has become almost irretrievably embroiled in sexual and racial politics. It is now almost always used to mean 'discrimination *against*'. Indeed, people, can now be *accused* of discrimination. From being almost synonymous with 'good judgement', then, this useful word has come, by overuse in a limited context, to be almost synonymous with 'prejudice'.

Let us also spare a thought for the much maligned and overused word *rhetoric*. Like 'discrimination', rhetoric is now almost invariably used in a derogatory sense. This was not always the case, however. Indeed, rhetoric was once considered an important part of any civilized person's education. Properly, rhetoric simply means the art of persuasive or impressive speaking or writing, and as such has a lot to do with wordpower.

A university student in the Middle Ages would have found that rhetoric was high on the list of subjects on his curriculum, and would also have found numerous treatises and dissertations on the subject in his university library. Modern teachers are in fact continuing the tradition of rhetoric when they tell their pupils that every essay must have an introduction, an argument and a conclusion, and most of the figures of speech we use today were given names by rhetoricians who lived hundreds of years ago. We still speak of 'a rhetorical question' when we mean a question to which an answer is not expected. Over the years, however, rhetoric, because of its concentration on the outward forms of speech and the way these forms can be used to persuade an audience, has come to be associated more and more with speeches on official or formal occasions – occasions, in fact, when the speaker, unless he or she is very unlucky, can rely on his or her captive audience not to argue back. When we hear in the press that a politician's address was 'mere rhetoric' we are left to assume from this that it was a speech full of high-flown phrases and empty promises, groundless and insincere.

Radio and television have played a major part in promoting the overuse of words and causing unfortunate changes in their meaning. This is particularly true of semi-technical words which, through the medium of weekly serials on subjects like nursing and crime detection, have come into popular usage in a very distorted form.

31

Take the sentence 'Forensic found traces of blood on his clothes'. *Forensic,* which features prominently in most detective stories, in fact means 'of or used in courts of law'. It does not in itself mean 'scientific', still less 'a team of scientists'. 'He had a cardiac' is equally meaningless. *Cardiac* is an adjective meaning 'of the heart' and can only be used as a noun to mean 'a person suffering from heart disease'. A cardiac *arrest* is a heart attack.

It is not only single words which suffer from overuse. You can also run yourself into trouble by using tags such as *if you like* and *as it were* too often. Such phrases have become the verbal equivalent of inverted commas around a word (see page 25) and can have the same effect. The dividing line between laudable reticence and lack of conviction is a fine one and phrases like these can be the deciding factor as to which side of the line you fall. *Actually* is another dangerous intruder. Always ask yourself if additions like these are really necessary. If they are not, don't use them; they will only detract from what you have to say.

Tautology

The overuse of words is closely associated with another, increasingly prevalent, misuse of words – tautology. Tautology is the practice of saying the same thing more than once in different ways. For example, look at the sentence you have just read. If it had read 'Tautology is the practice of saying the same thing repeatedly more than once in different ways' it would have been tautologous, because *repeatedly* and *more than once* mean the same thing. Now look at the following sentence:

> This directory contains a comprehensive listing of all the professional bodies in the audiovisual field.

This, as it stands, is tautologous (as is the statement 'This, as it stands, is tautologous'). The sentence must be rewritten either as

> This directory contains a listing of all the professional bodies in the audiovisual field.

or as

> This directory contains a comprehensive listing of the professional bodies in the audiovisual field.

If the listing is comprehensive it must contain all the professional bodies, and if all the professional bodies are there the listing must be comprehensive.

Tautology is a sure sign of muddled thinking, and, like most other misuses of words, is more serious when it occurs in written English than it is in spoken English. For example, the common tautologies *great big* and *tiny little* are generally acceptable in everyday speech (although they are now used so often that they carry no more weight than either *big, great, tiny* or *little* would carry separately). However, they would be out of place on a fairly formal occasion and would be quite inadmissible in serious writing.

Many tautologies have nonetheless crept into written English. It is not unusual to see someone or something described as *completely unique,* despite the fact that if anything is unique it is automatically completely so. 'Unique' is one of a number of words which are technically not comparable. Nothing can be 'relatively unique' or 'less unique'. Either it is unique or it is not – there is no halfway house. The same applies to words like *fundamental, empty, supreme, simultaneous, ultimate, absolute* and *perfect,* which are also often misused.

Advertising copywriters are, among others, great offenders in this sphere. To hammer home their message about the latest soap powder or CD player they will pile up not only superlatives but also the most shameless tautologies. Products are frequently described as 'the very best' in their field or as 'the ultimate in perfection'. One piece of advertising copy, designed to promote the wonders of a new deodorant, even spoke in seductive terms of 'the green forests of Scandinavia' (thus distinguishing them from the blue and red forests of Scandinavia to which your mind would otherwise have taken flight). If confronted with this, the writers concerned would no doubt excuse themselves on the grounds that they were seeking to create a *visual picture.*

News and current affairs programmes can also claim their share of tautologous usage. How many times have you heard about a 'serious crisis' or a 'terrible catastrophe' somewhere in the world? Tautology, from being a fault of style, has become the staple produce of sensationalism. This has had a very damaging effect upon language and, therefore, upon the way we think. Just as continual exposure to violence can harden you to the sight of it, so the media's bombardment of their public with tautologies has led to us no longer regarding a 'crisis' as important unless it is a *serious* crisis, and no longer paying much attention to a mere 'catastrophe' unless it is presented to us as a *terrible* one.

33

Certainly there are different levels of crisis and catastrophe, just as there are different degrees of excellence or danger. Certainly, too, it would be foolish to suggest that words like *disaster* or *tragedy* should never be given the extra emphasis of adjectives. It is simply unfortunate that once these emphatic additions become established you have to find more and more extreme ways of describing, for example, an earthquake which is genuinely worse than other earthquakes. Now that the rot has set in it is difficult to see quite how you can avoid helping it to spread.

The same is true of less dramatic tautologies. Many everyday phrases contribute to this cumulative devaluation of language. Take the phrase 'I have given your letter my careful consideration', which is a standard business formula. Anything less than *careful* consideration is now likely to be taken as a snub. But what does *consideration* mean if not 'careful thought'? Similarly, if everyone around you claims to be giving his or her 'considered opinion' on a particular topic, people may wonder whether your mere 'opinion' has been given more than a moment's thought. In some cases these unnecessary usages have led to the most ridiculous contortions of the English language. There was, for example, the government spokesman who made the extraordinary statement 'Some of the facts are true, some are distorted, and some are untrue'. Quite what an untrue fact is he failed to explain. And more recently there was the company secretary who, writing about changes in communication patterns, informed his readers, accurately enough but not very helpfully, that we now live in 'a truly global world'.

Tautology is also built into many figures of speech which were once used for emphasis but which have now, through overuse, become sterile and ineffective. Such tags include *each and every, as and when* and that particularly meaningless jingle *in any shape or form*. Some of these, such as *in this day and age,* have crossed the border into cliché (see page 39).

Tautologies such as these are largely perpetuated by the increasing convergence of spoken and written English. People are coming more and more to write as they speak, to put their thoughts straight on to paper, often without having worked them out thoroughly beforehand and without reading them through afterwards. And although no one would wish to open an unbridgeable gap between the way people speak and the way people write (even if such a gap were possible) the different conditions which apply to the way people read and the way people listen demand correspondingly different approaches.

To get your point across to a listener you will use all the

spontaneous means at your disposal, including hand movements and facial expressions. In the interests of effective communication it may sometimes, ironically, even be useful to say the same thing more than once in different ways (although this will obviously become counterproductive beyond a certain point). A reader, however, can reasonably expect you to express yourself more carefully and concisely in writing, and you, for your part, can reasonably expect a greater degree of concentration from a reader than from a listener. A reader will be irritated by tautologies and redundant phrases which a listener may well accept. Sentences which change direction in midstream can easily be forgiven when you are speaking. The same sentences on paper will always look like sloppy thinking. Tautologies are notoriously easy to overlook when you are writing. Always read through what you have written and make as many changes as are necessary in order to convey your meaning clearly and concisely.

Finally, there is a breed of tautology against which it is worth filing a special petition. Too many writers and speakers these days attempt to make their subjects sound more impressive by using more words than are strictly necessary. They will say that a problem has now 'diminished in magnitude' when they mean that it has got smaller; that a scheme was put into effect 'over a long period of time' when they mean that it was introduced gradually (*period of time* is always to be avoided); and that the 'geographical location' of an event was such-and-such when they mean that it took place there. Such phrases are not impressive. They simply display a lack of substance in what is being said.

Perhaps the most notorious of all these aggrandizing tags is the word *situation*. And it is with this unconcionably maltreated word that we enter the overpopulated province of jargon.

Jargon

Someone once said that in Chaucer's day (Chaucer died in 1400) a polyglot could have managed to read the world's entire published output within normal working hours. With sufficient languages at his command, then, a medieval scholar could theoretically have kept up to date with everything that was being written on every subject throughout the civilized world.

The expansion of human knowledge that has taken place since the fifteenth century has forced us into specialization. And today even a specialist in the most recondite academic discipline cannot hope to monitor every publication in his or her immediate field, still less to read everything that bears less directly upon it. By comparison, what we call 'general knowledge' is the merest scratching at a few of the surfaces of human knowledge. You have only to walk into your local library to realize the sheer weight of information on every conceivable topic that now confronts each of us. We are all forced to choose between knowing a reasonable amount about a very small area and knowing a very small amount about a number of areas. The structure of most jobs favours the first alternative; the media, by broadcasting information about the more accessible specialist subjects, attempt to redress the balance in favour of the second.

It is hardly surprising, therefore, that a species of vocabulary has developed which reflects the specialist nature of modern knowledge. One definition of jargon is 'a mode of speech familiar to a particular group or profession but not generally understood outside that group'. A layman, for example, would make little headway reading a scientific article on the photosynthesis of light or listening to a lecture on neuro-surgery, and one of the main reasons for this would be his or her inability to understand the terminology used.

There is, of course, nothing wrong with this sort of jargon. Chemical or medical terms are essential to the development of human under-standing as a whole, even if, in themselves, they are understood by only a very small proportion of the human race. No one would refuse to undergo a life-saving heart operation on the grounds that he or she did not know what an *aorta* is. Some things have to be taken on trust.

Nor is this brand of justifiable jargon confined to the scientific world. Take the subject of words, for example. You might be forgiven for thinking that, because you are sufficiently interested in words to have picked up this book in the first place, you should be able to make sense of most things that are written on this apparently quite accessible subject. Look, however, at the following discussion of pronunciation changes, which comes from a book called *Changing English* by Simeon Potter. The author is talking about the way we say the words *warmth, sense* and *length*:

> In passing from nasal plosive to breathed fricative you lower
> your velum a split second too soon and you inadvertently
> articulate a homorganic buccal plosive. This tendency to
> insert such *epenthetic* consonant sounds is a quite harmless
> one. It makes for greater ease in utterance and it is probably
> increasing.

Without a knowledge of the specialist terms concerned, you do not know whether to be encouraged or not by the fact that the changes the author mentions are 'harmless'.

Now look at the following passage. It comes from *The Mirror and the Lamp* by M H Abrams, and is a good example of the 'jargon' of a particular school of literary criticism.

> The dynamic conflict of opposites, and their reconciliation into a higher third, is not limited to the process of individual consciousness. The same concept serves Coleridge as the root-principle of his cosmogony, his epistemology and his theory of poetic creation alike . . . In Coleridge's criticism, accordingly, the imaginative synthesis of discordant or antithetic aesthetic qualities replaces Wordsworth's 'nature' as the criterion of highest poetic value; and this on grounds inherent in Coleridge's world-view.

You will notice that here we have entered a different area of jargon. Whereas in the passage from Simeon Potter our understanding of the author's thought is blocked by our ignorance of his specialist terms, the language here is *not* specialist language. You may have to look up a few words like *cosmogony* and *epistemology* but, to be understood, the passage as a whole does not require any specialist knowledge. It simply requires time and effort. What obstructs our immediate understanding is not the words themselves but the way they are used – the overall 'flavour' of the passage.

The passage from *The Mirror and the Lamp* comes dangerously close to being jargon in the sense in which we normally use the word. It would be unfair to suggest that the passage is meaningless or simply pretentious, but one cannot help wondering whether the author might not have written it in a slightly more approachable way.

One of the main dangers with this type of jargon is that the regular association of certain words and phrases with certain contexts can remove the need for careful thought about what is actually being said. And it is continual reappraisal of what words mean and of the way they are used that prevents language from stagnating, and ultimately makes accurate expression possible.

When we speak of jargon we usually mean language which is obscure and pretentious, and which uses complicated words and constructions where simpler ones would do. In particular we tend to think of the sort of jargon that is used in the business world (and especially in marketing), the bureaucratic world, the media and certain academic disciplines such as the social sciences. This too is often unfair, but one cannot help suspecting on occasions that the most dedicated jargon-mongers in these fields share the attitude of the character in Gilbert and Sullivan's *Patience* who sings:

> If this young man expresses himself
> In terms too deep for me,
> Why, what a very very deep young man
> This deep young man must be!

Jargon seems often to be used to maintain the mystique of a job or profession, to set it apart from the 'ordinary'. It is something most of us are guilty of at some time or other. We use words not to communicate but to sound impressive, to show how knowledgeable we are about our own particular specialisms. And it is only too easy to carry this over into writing, especially when we have least to say. Jargon is a notorious padder-out of lean ideas.

Which brings us back to *situation*. The *Concise Oxford Dictionary* defines it as 'Place, with its surroundings, occupied by something (*house stands in a fine situation*); set of circumstances, position in which one finds oneself (*came out of a difficult situation with credit*) . . . ' It is the second of these definitions which suffers the greatest abuse. Nowadays, despite the concentrated ridicule of jargon-spotters, 'situation' is frequently seen in the company of nouns masquerading as adjectives when there is really no call for it to be around at all. For example, 'These tests may be administered in a classroom situation' means nothing more than 'These tests may be administered in the classroom'. Similarly, 'This organization is now in a non-growth situation' simply means 'This organization is not growing'. In both cases, the use of the world 'situation' lends an air of false impressiveness to the idea. More recently, as if 'situation' itself were now lacking in impressiveness, *situational context* has begun to appear. This is surely to progress from a frying pan situation into the situational context of the fire.

Other pseudo-impressive words are also in vogue. *Viable* for 'feasible' or 'practicable' has already been mentioned (see page 30). *Utilize*, which means no more than 'use', has become so firmly rooted that it now seems likely to remain with us for much longer than it deserves. *Parameter,* recently snatched from the precise world of mathematics, is now used so often to mean 'boundary' or 'framework' that it is in danger of being mistaken for *perimeter*. And it is high time *ongoing*, as a synonym for 'continual', onwent.

Why do so many people feel an overpowering need to aggrandize the commonplace as if there were something shameful about it? Why do spokesmen, reporters, managers, football commentators (the list is endless) have to say *at this particular moment in time* when it takes less breath and effort to say *now*? Why say *I react very negatively to that* when you mean you don't like it at all? If a statement or idea is commonplace, no putting out of more verbal flags can disguise the fact, still less change it. Jargon is like the sustaining pedal on the piano. It is often used in an attempt to mask a bad performance but serves only to point it up.

Some uses of jargon are not merely loose or unnecessary but wrong. For example, it would be unfortunate if the usage 'update me on that one' became accepted. You may be able to update a set of facts but you cannot update a person. Again, a group of people can agree *to* a proposal. They can even agree *on* a proposal. But they cannot 'agree a proposal'. You can be the head of a department. You can even, at a pinch, head that department. But you cannot – or at least you ought not to be able to – 'head it up'. And once you are there, you would be much better advised to make firm proposals than to make infirm ones and 'firm them up' later.

It would also make for an easier life if nouns remained nouns and verbs remained verbs unless there was good reason for them not to. There is surely no good reason for saying 'We have to *trend* these figures' or 'This is a difficult case to *profile*'. And why assess 'the total marketing *spend*'? You don't get charged in a restaurant for your 'total eat'.

Unnecessary jargon impinges on our everyday life and language without enriching or expanding either. In many cases it sets precedents which it would be a pity to follow. Methodical thinking almost always leads to economical writing. The tendency of too much of our jargon, however, is towards long-windedness and redundant usage. And this, reflecting in turn upon the way we think, is apt, in the jargon of transactional analysis, to imply a somewhat not-OK ego-state.

Clichés

The word cliché comes from the French verb *clicher* meaning to make a metal casting of a stereotype. It is used in English to mean an outworn or hackneyed expression.

It is extraordinarily difficult to avoid using clichés in speech and writing. They present themselves at every turn, begging for employment. *The point is* (there's one of them) that such expressions have very often become clichés precisely because they are so apt. The more they are used, however, the more ineffective they become, until eventually they are not only meaningless but laughable.

Below is a list of 50 clichés which are still in daily use despite the fact that their edges are becoming increasingly blunt.

add insult to injury
as a matter of fact
avoid like the plague
be that as it may
bite the bullet
born and bred
the bottom line
burn the midnight oil
chop and change
conspicuous by its absence
to cut a long story short
the dim and distant past
easier said than done
every effort is being made to . . .
explore every avenue
far and wide
far be it from me to . . .
few and far between
first and foremost
for the foreseeable future
it goes without saying (so why say it?)
golden opportunity
go the whole hog
have a bone to pick with
if the worst comes to the worst
in no uncertain terms
in the nick of time
in a nutshell
it stands to reason
kill two birds with one stone
last but not least
the last straw
a moot point (sometimes misrepresented as 'a mute point'!)
on the spur of the moment
on the tip of my tongue

or words to that effect (a particularly dangerous cliché for anyone
    laying claim to wordpower!)
pass the buck
the powers that be
pure and simple
reading between the lines
really and truly
rough and ready
slowly but surely
stick your neck out
a storm in a teacup
a sweeping statement
take the rough with the smooth
to all intents and purposes
a tower of strength
turn a blind eye

Obviously, there will be occasions when no harm will be done by
using any of these. The danger is that, because these phrases are so
commonly seen and heard, they will be used when fresher phrases
might better serve the purpose. Clichés can easily become a habit and
are apt to lead to laziness in thought, speech and writing. The tag *in
this day and age* has already been mentioned (see page 34) as being
particularly meaningless. It is often used merely as a synonym for
nowadays, and very much more often simply to pad out a statement or
sentence (a fault many clichés share with jargon). Other clichés
which serve no useful purpose (and, indeed, often call their users'
sincerity into question) are the introductory phrases *I hate to mention
it but* . . . and *to tell you the truth. Far be it from me to* . . . , listed above,
almost always means precisely the opposite of what it claims to mean.
    Many clichés have become such because they refer to circum-
stances or states of mind which are familiar to all of us. Such
expressions are in many ways the most dangerous clichés of all
because they can easily become a substitute for original thought. For
example, the phrase 'This is the happiest day of my life' has now been
so thoroughly overworked that, even when it is true, it sounds
perfunctory. Similarly, *my heart bleeds for you* (once, no doubt, a very
colourful phrase) is now apt to sound insincere or even sarcastic. Nor
does it sound particularly convincing any more to say that someone
has a heart of gold or *stands head and shoulders above the rest*. It is, generally,
worth thinking twice before using any phrase that is beginning to
show signs of exhaustion from overwork.

A number of phrases became popular because of their vividness and then became clichés because of their popularity. It is a pity that *lay it on with a trowel* (which occurs in Shakespeare's *As You Like it*) has now become something of a cliché. The same is true of *bloated plutocrat* which must once have had a comparable visual impact. *High and dry* is another sad loss to the world of respectable metaphor. Other expressions which fall into this regrettable category are *grasp the nettle, you've hit the nail on the head, in the heat of the moment, the life and soul of the party* and *the luck of the devil*. Most of these are still usable in spoken English (though they ring rather hollow even there) but look stale in writing.

Proverbs have supplied us with many clichés. *A bird in the hand, too many cooks, the blind leading the blind, a stitch in time* and many others have now lost much of their original edge. Some phrases have escaped from their proverbs and taken on a life of their own, only to become clichés in the process. For example, *a friend in need* which, in the proverb 'a friend in need is a friend indeed', means 'someone who is a friend to you when you are in need' is now often used in isolation to mean 'a friend of yours who is in need'. It is extremely difficult to give proverbial clichés a new lease of life. In *The Mayor of Casterbridge* Thomas Hardy writes 'a maxim glibly repeated from childhood remains practically unmarked till some mature experience enforces it'. True though this is, it is still virtually impossible to convey that mature experience to somebody else by means of the original maxim.

Another, closely related, family of clichés traces its origins to great works of literature. From the Bible come *turn the other cheek, go from strength to strength, grind the faces of the poor, the land of the living* and (to quote another cliché) others too numerous to mention. More still come from Shakespeare, sometimes directly, sometimes by misquotation. Among these are *salad days (Anthony and Cleopatra), in my mind's eye (Hamlet), at one fell swoop (Macbeth), foregone conclusion (Othello)* and *hoist with his own petard (Hamlet)*. Alexander Pope has given us *damn with faint praise* and William Cowper *monarch of all I survey*. All these are too hackneyed to be usable in serious writing, and it is anyway more often an admission of failure than a tribute to resort to another author's exact words.

Other clichés can be classified as euphemisms – that is, they are oblique references to subjects over which, to quote one of their number, we feel we should *draw a veil*. Not surprisingly, a number of these clichés reflect social taboos such as sex (*ladies of the night, bestowed her favours, just good friends,* etc) and death (*gone to a better place, departed this life, passed away,* etc). Others reflect, one suspects, widely shared insecurities – for example, *thin on top* for 'going bald'.

The world of sport is another fertile breeding ground for clichés. Press, radio and television coverage of most sporting activities has created almost unaided the characteristic language of sporting commentary and broadcast it to vast numbers of people. The clichés here result partly from a need for variety. In soccer, for example, *a peach of a shot* can either be *powered in* or *driven home* or, if neither of these will serve, *slotted away* without anybody questioning the difference. The player who scored will in any case be *a very happy man* or even, if not restrained, *over the moon*.

Nor is it only in the sporting world that clichés can lead to absurdity. Some become absurd by misuse, as in the case of the trade union representative who complained that the management had 'pulled the bread and butter from under his feet' or the hi-fi salesman who explained that the quality of loudspeakers is 'largely in the ear of the beholder'.

And, as a final warning against the indiscriminate use of clichés, remember the story of the show business personality who was asked to be the godfather of a colleague's child. On inquiring the name of his godson-to-be, he was told that the baby was to be christened John. 'John?', he replied with evident distaste, 'But every Tom, Dick and Harry's called John!'

Ambiguity

Ambiguity is the presence of two or more different meanings in a single word, phrase or combination of phrases. It is also the sworn enemy of accurate communication and one of the commonest betrayers of muddled thinking.

Wordpower is very much a matter of arranging words so as to exclude from them the meanings you do not intend them to convey. (An example of the way in which grammatical rules can help you to achieve the most appropriate arrangement of words was given on page 27). Unfortunately, it is very easy to overlook ambiguities, largely because when you are speaking or writing you generally have a fairly clear idea of what you are speaking or writing about and it is therefore easy to assume that, because *you* know what you mean, your listener or reader will also know. The problem is made more acute by the fact that many words and phrases in the English language do not have a single clear meaning. Look, for example, at the sentence you have just read. It contains the ambiguous statement many words and phrases in the English language do not have a single clear meaning.

This could mean either

many words and phrases in the English language have a number of meanings, none of which is clear in itself

or

many words and phrases in the English language have more than one meaning.

The context in which the sentence appears will have given you some clues to the fact that the second meaning was the one intended, but it will not have given you enough to rule out the possibility of the first alternative.

It is never possible to do away with ambiguity altogether; even the most accomplished writers and speakers sometimes lapse into it. Nor would it be desirable to do so, because ambiguity and richness are two sides of the same linguistic coin. Much of our greatest literature (and particularly our greatest poetry) depends upon controlled ambiguity for its full effect. Language and thought are not one and the same, and words can only approximate to what we think or feel. But if, as we are always being told, we are rational animals, we should be able to make that approximation as close a one as possible. The problem of ambiguity is an important aspect of wordpower precisely because it is the problem of language in miniature. And that problem is the problem of getting thoughts from one mind to another without too much being lost along the way.

A soldier returns from the war. His civilian friends ask him 'Where were you wounded?' He does not know whether to answer 'In the leg' or 'Just outside Ypres'. Each of the soldier's friends wil know the type of answer he or she expects, and as far as each of them is concerned 'Where were you wounded?' is the right question to elicit that answer. The only access the soldier has to their thoughts, however, is through the phrasing of their questions.

Similarly, the question 'When did you decide to go to France?' can either be answered 'Yesterday' or 'Next June' according to whether you think it means 'When did you make the decision?' or 'When are you going?' Application forms for jobs are often equally ambiguous in their wording. What, for example, do you write in the box marked

FAMILY? As is often the case, ambiguity and inefficiency here go hand in hand. By failing to narrow the range of possible responses, the compilers of the form concerned no doubt received a large number of answers which told them either more or less than they wanted to know.

Always try to put yourself in the position of the person you are speaking or writing to. And, if you are writing, always read through what you have written. It is only to easy to lose your way in the middle of what you are saying, and to find, on reading it through afterwards, that what seemed crystal clear at the time has somehow become confused in the process of committing it to paper. If necessary start all over again, using what you have written as a first draft. The wide availability of the wordprocessor has made it much easier to draft and redraft in this way without wasting reams of paper and hours of time.

Beware of using qualifying words like *certain* and *apparent* if you want to avoid ambiguity. 'He had a certain claim to the land' can mean either 'His claim to the land was an incontrovertible one' or 'He had some sort of claim to the land'. 'Her apparent stupidity led to her dismissal' could mean that she seemed stupid but wasn't or that her stupidity was obvious to everyone. Make sure, too, that adjectives and adverbs clearly relate to the nouns and verbs you intend them to relate to. 'Alfred's hair needs cutting badly' could mean that Alfred's hair is of the rare kind that would benefit from the services of a really appalling barber, whereas 'Alfred's hair badly needs cutting' removes the ambiguity. Again, 'The Government aims to help small shopkeepers' is unlikely to mean that shopkeepers over five foot six need not apply for assistance.

Signs and notices have become increasingly cryptic in recent years – sometimes, indeed, to the point of absurdity. The sign SEWAGE DISPOSAL WORKS is unlikely to be greeted with a relieved 'I'm very pleased to hear it'. But the notice KING CHARLES COLOURED POSTCARDS which appeared over the bookstall in a country church once visited by that monarch must have left many people wondering at the thoroughness of historical research and the mundane hobbies of seventeenth-century royalty.

Such counterproductive compression is no doubt partly the legacy of 'headline English', examples of which can be found in any modern newspaper. Journalists, like poets and politicians, often turn the inbuilt ambiguities of language to their own advantage. An eyecatching headline whose meaning is not immediately clear invariably lures the reader to buy and find out more.

But 'headline English' should be confined to headlines. The piles of nouns which characterize this form of writing (NEW YORK VICE KING PROBE, PARIS WOMAN STABBING MYSTERY) serve only to hinder accurate communication. And verbs, long considered the most important parts of speech, seem to be in short supply among headline writers – perhaps because when they do appear they can be disastrously ambiguous. It is, after all, a curious verbal country where commuters can be hit by cancelled trains.

PART TWO: THE TESTS

3. Introduction to the tests

The rest of this book is made up of word tests of various kinds. The tests are divided into three general categories: spelling tests, definition tests and tests of usage and verbal reasoning.

Each of the tests is prefaced by a brief introduction considering the particular aspect or aspects of wordpower it is designed to draw attention to, and, in some cases, suggesting the sort of situation in which a development of that type of wordpower might prove to be a valuable asset. Instructions on how to do the tests are also given in these sections.

Some of the tests, especially in the verbal reasoning section, are modelled on those used by employers to assess the wordpower of potential employees. In these cases you should, where indicated in the introductory section, set yourself a time limit within which to do as much of the test as you can. The reason for doing these tests against the clock is that they are designed largely to test the speed at which you work things out and make connections between words and ideas.

The questions in each of the tests get harder as the test goes on, and the last questions in each test are sometimes very difficult. You may find that you have given a lot of wrong answers, but then the tests would hardly be very useful or enjoyable if you could skip through them and get everything right without having to think at all.

Answers to all the tests are provided at the end of the book (pages 115–122), but you will not find any scoring system based on these answers. It is not the aim of *Wordpower* to provide an elaborate system of self-assessment based on your results in these tests because such a system would not be particularly useful. Where verbal tests are used by employers they almost always form part of a complete test battery designed to test a number of aspects of the employee's or potential employee's general aptitude. From these wide-ranging results a profile of the person concerned can be drawn up and areas of latent ability can be identified. The candidate's potential can then be developed in these areas.

The tests in this book are certainly of a practical nature, but they are, of course, concerned only with wordpower. Although, as we have seen, an ability to use words correctly and efficiently is a crucial qualification in many spheres of activity, it does not necessarily imply anything about your ability in such areas as numeracy, spatial awareness or mechanical reasoning. It would therefore be misleading to draw broad conclusions about your general aptitude from your scores in these tests. From reading the first part of the book, however, you will already have developed some idea of the areas in which wordpower is important and of how these areas relate to your own field of experience.

The most important thing is that these tests should stimulate and expand your interest in, and understanding of, words and the way they work. You will already have some awareness of the many uses and misuses of words and of the traps they continually lay for the unwary. These tests will help you to consolidate that awareness, to find where your personal strengths lie and where, perhaps, there is room for further improvement.

Have fun.

4. Spelling tests

Words out of context

How often have you written a word and then stared at it until you could no longer say whether or not it was correctly spelt? Most people have their blind spots when it comes to spelling. There are probably words whose spelling you have looked up time after time in the dictionary but can still never be sure about when you come to write them down. The correct and incorrect versions are so mixed up in your mind that you can no longer tell which is which.

Perhaps some of these words may appear in the tests which follow. In this first test you are presented with a list of words which are commonly misspelt. Two versions of each word are given. One is spelt correctly, the other is not. Note beside each pair of words the letter (A or B) which corresponds to the correctly spelt version. When you have finished the whole test, check your answers with those given on page 115.

(1)	A. necessary	B. neccessary	_____
(2)	A. separate	B. seperate	_____
(3)	A. paralell	B. parallel	_____
(4)	A. ceiling	B. cieling	_____
(5)	A. sieze	B. seize	_____
(6)	A. privilege	B. priviledge	_____
(7)	A. tomatos	B. tomatoes	_____
(8)	A. withold	B. withhold	_____
(9)	A. compulsory	B. compulsary	_____
(10)	A. definate	B. definite	_____

(11) A. ommitted   B. omitted   _____

(12) A. bachelor   B. batchelor   _____

(13) A. embarassed   B. embarrassed   _____

(14) A. rhythm   B. rythm   _____

(15) A. manoeuvre   B. manouvre   _____

(16) A. harrass   B. harass   _____

(17) A. occurred   B. occured   _____

(18) A. thouroughfare   B. thoroughfare   _____

(19) A. committee   B. commitee   _____

(20) A. commitment   B. committment   _____

(21) A. impostor   B. imposter   _____

(22) A. giraffe   B. girraffe   _____

(23) A. accommodate   B. accomodate   _____

(24) A. indispensible   B. indispensable   _____

(25) A. Mediterranean   B. Meditterranean   _____

(26) A. beaurocracy   B. bureaucracy   _____

(27) A. guarantee   B. gaurantee   _____

(28) A. unwieldy   B. unweildy   _____

(29) A. encyclopedia   B. encyclopeadia   _____

(30) A. miscellaneous   B. miscellaeneous   _____

(31) A. miniscule   B. minuscule   _____

(32) A. desiccate   B. dessicate   _____

(33) A. superintendant   B. superintendent   _____

(34) A. auxillary   B. auxiliary   _____

(35) A. acquiescent   B. aquiescent   _____

(36) A. consciencious   B. conscientious   _____

(37) A. asinine   B. assinine   _____

(38) A. ashphalt   B. asphalt   _____

(39) A. Mississippi   B. Misissippi   _____

(40) A. supersede   B. supercede   _____

(41) A. liquefy   B. liquify   _____

(42) A. homogenous   B. homogeneous   _____

(43) A. anemone   B. anenome   _____

(44) A. licquor   B. liquor   _____

(45) A. langorous   B. languorous   _____

(46) A. rarefy   B. rarify   _____

(47) A. pejorative   B. perjorative   _____

(48) A. concensus   B. consensus   _____

(49) A. elegiac   B. elegaic   _____

(50) A. braggadocio   B. braggadoccio   _____

Words in context

In the following test you are given a number of sentences. In each of the sentences there is *one* word spelt incorrectly. Pick out the word in each sentence that you think is incorrect and write the correct spelling in the space provided. When you have finished the whole test check your answers with those given on page 115.

---

(1) The gorrilla was housed in a cage near the rhinoceros.

   _____

(2) 'For the fourtieth time, there isn't room for two pianos in this house.'

   _____

(3) James put every conceivable hinderance in his opponent's way.

   _____

(4) 'I can say without exageration that my asthma has never been this bad before.'

   _____

(5) The restaurant served its clientele with flaggons of cider.

   _____

(6) He regarded his fear of the dark as a serious psychological abberation.

   _____

(7) He caught a chill while scuba-diving and it lead to laryngitis.

_____

(8) The trellis along which the roses were trained was attached to the lathe and plaster wall of the cottage.

_____

(9) The owner of the off-licence was remarkably knowledgable about liqueurs.

_____

(10) Drawing a line between deference and obsequeousness is a perennial difficulty.

_____

(11) No traveller has ever unraveled the mystery of the sphinx.

_____

(12) Curing the sick opossum tested Eric's vetinary skills to the limit.

_____

(13) During her pregnancy Judy developed cravings for gherkins and pomegranites.

_____

(14) As time went on and they drank more of the landlord's strongest beer their gaity became positively frolicsome.

_____

(15) She remarked drily that James was underated by other people only because he had such a low opinion of his own abilities.

_____

(16) He tried to smoothe the surface but could not achieve any degree of evenness.

_____

(17) Policemen became suspicious of the aircraft mechanics when they were discovered ferretting about in the hangar.

_____

(18) Despite his laxity in other matters, John's guardian drew the line at cleptomania.

_____

(19) The jist of his argument was that the lieutenant should guard the barricade.

_____

(20) Henry's obstreperous niece has chillblains, and serve her right!

_____

(21) Janet's hairbrained scheme to renovate the entire premises was laughed at by everyone present.

_____

(22) Some people believe it's sacreligious to trespass on consecrated ground.

_____

(23) He had received largesse from his neighbours for years, but his own meaness was indisputable.

_____

(24) The meteorological office had forecast hailstorms and torrential rain but had made no mention of thunder and lightening.

_____

(25) The pet-shop proprietor doubted whether the guineau-pig was saleable.

_____

(26) The filiment spread its hazy incandescence through the darkened room.

_____

(27) Today he is chiefly remembered for having committed greusome *hara-kiri* before a crowd of hundreds.

_____

(28) 'I'm afraid I shall have to forego the pleasure of your company tonight because I have already been inveigled into going to the opera with Sir Harold.'

_____

(29) We condone the seizure of funds procured by heroine trafficking.

_____ .

(30) The differences between genuine rococo statues and the replicas in this pavillion are negligible.

_____

(31) The bursar read us an excerpt from the ficticious adventures of Tom Jones.

_____

(32) Sue planted celeriac next to the lettuces on the allottment.

_____

(33) Even in this idylic spot his mind turned to thoughts of vengeance.

_____

(34) Volcanos are honeycombed with subterranean labyrinths.

_____

(35) Despite the government's attempts to extirpate it altogether, scurrilous literature has proved an intractible problem.

_____

(36) Mrs Robinson remained sanguin about the fuchsia's chances of survival, despite the fact that the peony was wilting.

_____

(37) Experience had inured him to the idea of receiving no recompence for his loss.

_____

(38) The tennis player surreptitiously swapped raquets after the first set.

_____

(39) Kate's principal idiosyncracy was a passion for marionettes.

_____

(40) Their Moroccan tour began inauspiciously with Jane suffering from catarrh and Francis suffering from diahorrea.

_____

5. Definition tests

Words from the news

Just as it is often the simplest foreign words for which a translator finds it most difficult to give an accurate English equivalent, so, in English, it is often the words we encounter quite frequently that we find it most difficult accurately to define. This is especially true of the sort of words which crop up regularly in newspaper, radio and television reports. It is only too easy to assume that you know the meaning of a word simply because the context in which it appears is a familiar one. It is not always so easy to give a satisfactory definition of that word when the context is taken away.

It is also very easy to read a newspaper article or listen to a broadcast news report without bringing your full concentration to bear upon the subject under discussion. How often, for example, do you find yourself reading a newspaper on a train with half an eye on the view outside the window or on the person sitting opposite? Again, how often do you use radio or television merely as a background to household activities such as cooking or cleaning?

The vast developments within the media, and particularly in radio and television, over the past few decades have made accessible to a wide public a number of areas of current interest which were formerly largely the province of the specialist. Nowadays, for example, we are continually bombarded with information about the world economic situation, but it is not many years since even such terms as 'inflation' and 'recession' were known and understood only by a relatively small group of people, such as economists and businessmen. Even today, when such terms are common currency, many of us might still stumble over the technical distinctions between 'deflation' and 'depreciation'.

All the words in the following test occur frequently in reports on current affairs, and should therefore, in theory at least, be among the most 'familiar' words in the language. When you see them out of context, however, you may be surprised to find that they are not as familiar as you thought. Each word is followed by four definitions, only one of which is correct. Make a note of the letter which corresponds to what you think is the right definition in each case and, when you have finished the whole test, check your answers with those given on page 116.

(1) **coercion**
A. government by force B. take-over bid C. joining of two political parties D. alliance between powers

(2) **armistice**
A. act of hostility B. arms limitation treaty C. truce D. memorial service

(3) **deterrent**
A. nuclear armament B. threat C. restraining by fear D. cleaning agent

(4) **nationalize**
A. change one's nationality B. convert into state property C. subsidize D. make redundant

(5) **totalitarianism**
A. dictatorial government by a single party B. tolerance of all parties C. state ownership of property D. government by the people

(6) **reactionary**
A. one who initiates change B. one who believes in freedom of speech C. solving problems as they arise D. one who opposes change

(7) **ratify**
A. invalidate B. confirm an agreement C. explain D. puzzle

(8) **to lobby**
A. to seek to influence B. to insult C. to present legislation D. to harass in public

(9) **coup d'état**
A. assassination B. violent change of government C. invasion of neighbouring territory D. sudden attack from the air

(10) **rationale**
A. promise made in manifesto B. fundamental reason
C. sensible policy D. political aim

(11) **proxy**
A. one authorized to act on another's behalf B. election
campaign C. one who misrepresents another's actions D. postal
vote

(12) **obsolescent**
A. disgusting B. not transparent C. not yet fully developed
D. going out of date

(13) **endemic**
A. disease B. peculiar to a certain area C. uncontrollable D. rife

(14) **referendum**
A. important issue B. statement of policy C. vote taken by the
people D. second opinion

(15) **caveat**
A. warning B. neckerchief C. administrative assembly D. leave
of absence

(16) **franchise**
A. authorization to sell goods B. economic restriction
C. trademark D. investment in industry

(17) **specious**
A. insulting B. belonging to a single type C. argumentative
D. only superficially plausible

(18) **guerrilla**
A. deserter B. revolutionary C. irregular combatant D. warfare
over a restricted area

(19) **entente**
A. intention B. commencement of hostilities C. friendly
understanding between states D. state of war

(20) **fiscal**
A. religious B. financial C. related to foreign affairs
D. diplomatic

(21) **renegade**
A. dissolute person B. turncoat C. small military unit D. one
who has been demoted

(22) **logistics**
A. art of moving troops B. armaments C. important questions
D. grounds for an opinion

(23) **polemic**
A. manifesto B. controversial exposition C. violent speech
D. explanation of action

(24) **archipelago**
A. labour camp B. group of islands C. constellation D. leader of
minority party

(25) **atrophy**
A. waste away B. military honour C. high praise D. lack of
interest

(26) **communiqué**
A. ambassador B. trade delegate C. official report D. newsflash

(27) **affidavit**
A. summons to appear in court B. written statement used as
evidence C. exemption from jury service D. papal blessing

(28) **détente**
A. treaty B. disarmament C. political tension D. easing of
strained relations

(29) **suffrage**
A. charge levied at ports B. oppression C. right to vote
D. political system which excludes women from office

(30) **tariff**
A. ban on imports B. right to trade C. insurance cover D. duties
on imports or exports

(31) **plutocracy**
A. system of promotion by merit B. government by
parliamentary assembly C. rule by the wealthy D. secret society

(32) **bicameral**
A. having two sessions every year B. consisting of two chambers
C. agreed between two parties D. of only passing interest

(33) **plenary**
A. meeting as and when required B. to be attended by all
members C. decision-making D. financial

(34) **cholesterol**
A. steroid alcohol found in body cells B. type of vegetable fat
C. gallery in church D. atmospheric pollutant

(35) **nadir**
A. highest point B. lowest point C. midway point D. Indian official

(36) **embargo**
A. termination of diplomatic relations B. declaration of martial law C. suspension of a branch of commerce D. additional tax on imported goods

(37) **catalyst**
A. member of terrorist organization B. nuclear explosion
C. natural catastrophe D. agent of change

(38) **unilateral**
A. concerning all parties B. unconditional C. affecting only one party D. to be put into effect in several stages

(39) **moratorium**
A. temporary prohibition B. public vote C. family tomb
D. consultation between senior officials

(40) **ballistic**
A. armed with nuclear warhead B. high-speed C. moving under force of gravity D. jet-propelled

(41) **recidivist**
A. one who believes in private enterprise B. one who relapses into crime C. one who takes bribes D. one who goes back on his or her word

(42) **peripatetic**
A. circular B. on the outskirts C. authoritarian D. going from place to place

(43) **cabal**
A. armed rebellion B. political clique C. private militia
D. unofficial industrial action

(44) **panegyric**
A. large lorry B. speech of praise C. firework D. funeral oration

(45) **pariah**
A. administrative area B. religious leader C. authoritarian governor D. social outcast

(46) **junta**

A. political faction after revolution B. uprising under military leadership C. right to veto a motion in parliament D. state dependent upon another

(47) **oligarchy**

A. government by a small group B. government by the majority C. one-party system D. two-party system

(48) **filibuster**

A. obstruct by prolonged speaking B. arms smuggler C. troubleshooter D. mercenary soldier

(49) **nexus**

A. decline of a party B. ruling group C. stalemate D. linked group

(50) **cadre**

A. convert to political cause B. member of communist unit C. army chaplain D. non-commissioned officer

Words from works of literature

Language changes and develops according to the way it is used by people in their daily lives. But these changes are both influenced and consolidated by the way in which forms of language are written down and passed on from one generation to the next. The books we read exert a powerful influence on the way we use words in our everyday business.

The most enduring channels through which language is passed down the generations are the great works of literature. No one but the occasional scholar now reads the daily newspapers of 1849, but almost everyone is familiar with Charles Dickens' great novel *David Copperfield* (which was written in that year), and although most of us have at some stage cursed 'Shakespeare's English' (as if it were somehow a deliberate attempt to confuse us!) you have only to read a few pages of *Hamlet* to see how many of the words and phrases we use every day derive from the work of this single extraordinary man.

It is one of the functions of literature, then, to reflect and develop the language of its time. Writers have more time to seek and find the right words for what they want to say than, for example, people speaking to their bosses on internal telephones, and if the writers are living up to their responsibilities they have a right to expect a similar degree of care from their readers. It is an unfortunate fact of life, however, that there is seldom time to exercise this care in reading a book. Certainly no one could be expected to read the sentences of a Flaubert or James Joyce with the same degree of concentration as that with which they were written, and, as far as unfamiliar words are concerned, it is not always convenient or desirable to have to keep referring to a dictionary while reading a book for pleasure.

Nonetheless, it is an interesting exercise to take a book you have already read and to go back over a chapter or two noting down the words whose meanings you are not absolutely certain about. You may find that the list is a little longer than you anticipated.

All the words in the test which follows are taken from the first few pages of famous works of literature. As in the 'Words from the news' test, each word is followed by four definitions, only one of which is correct. Note down the letter which corresponds to what you think is the right definition in each case, and when you have finished the whole test, check your answers with those given on page 116. (You will also find there the name of the book in which the word appears. If you have read the book you should have known the word. Did you?)

---

(1) **bigotry**
A. double marriage B. adoration C. prostitution D. prejudice

(2) **sanguine**
A. bloodstained B. hopeful C. easily annoyed D. related

(3) **contentious**
A. irritable B. controversial C. happy D. violent

(4) **expostulated**
A. made protest B. explained C. exclaimed D. argued

(5) **perennial**
A. annual B. lasting for ever C. on the outskirts D. habitual

(6) **loquacious**
A. fluid B. pompous C. insincere D. talkative

(7) **esoteric**
A. not generally intelligible B. exotic C. self-centred D. self-defeating

(8) **patriarchal**
A. venerable B. aristocratic C. loving one's homeland D. authoritative

(9) **plagiaristic**
A. servile B. aggressive C. given to stealing others' ideas D. given to favouring one's relations

(10) **trousseau**
A. bouquet B. bridal outfit C. small bread roll D. trifling matter

(11) **stucco**
A. cement coating B. stiletto C. orchestral passage D. brickwork

(12) **pecuniary**
A. unusual B. impoverished C. related to money D. miserly

(13) **rapacity**
A. greed B. speed C. cruelty D. lust

(14) **stevedores**
A. acrobats B. ship-loaders C. unemployed men D. small-town adventurers

(15) **opacity**
A. lewdness B. fatness C. opaqueness D. greed

(16) **votaries**
A. prayers B. burnt offerings C. candidates for election D. devotees

(17) **eclectic**
A. borrowing from various sources B. happy-go-lucky C. living as a hermit D. producing a violent reaction

(18) **circumambulate**
A. talk at length B. hesitate C. walk around D. surround

(19) **attenuated**
A. rarefied B. forgiven C. implied D. unconvincing

(20) **umbrageous**
A. brooding B. boastful C. unforgivable D. shady

(21) **immolated**
A. weakened B. burnt C. sacrificed D. immersed in water

(22) **excrescence**
A. outgrowth B. revulsion C. dung D. exclusion

(23) **orthography**
A. normal belief B. correct spelling C. map-making D. the art of drawing birds

(24) **cavillers**
A. swordsmen B. gossips C. wrongdoers D. objectors

(25) **ferrule**
A. stiff collar B. metal ring C. small missile D. furlined overcoat

(26) **recalcitrance**
A. cruelty B. repentance C. obstinacy D. chalkiness

(27) **echelon**
A. coat of arms B. badge C. rank D. V-shaped formation

67

(28) **demotic**
A. tyrannical B. imitative C. mad D. popular

(29) **farrago**
A. medley B. uproar C. coach D. crowd

(30) **jejune**
A. small boiled sweet B. naive C. senile D. crafty

(31) **carmine**
A. rifle B. gathering of troops C. crimson D. of the flesh

(32) **lucubrations**
A. lengthy explanations B. oilings C. nocturnal meditations
D. consequences

(33) **sienna**
A. mountain range B. Spanish governess C. brown pigment
D. grassland

(34) **pedagogic**
A. powerful B. ancestral C. schoolmasterly D. worshipping
many gods

(35) **moiety**
A. inheritance B. one of two parts C. sadness D. abundance

(36) **salinity**
A. dirtiness B. saltiness C. healthiness D. lechery

(37) **huckster**
A. gambler B. pedlar C. small shopkeeper D. cheat

(38) **prolix**
A. fluent B. generous C. lustful D. tediously wordy

(39) **termagant**
A. seabird B. burrowing insect C. overbearing woman D. one
who objects to a will

(40) **bourdon**
A. bundle B. low organ stop C. chorus D. lament

(41) **homunculus**
A. great-uncle B. miniature man C. type of fungus
D. philosopher

(42) **whangee**
A. whisky-based cocktail B. open carriage C. excursion
D. bamboo cane

(43) **biretta**
A. dagger B. type of lizard C. square cap D. peasant tunic

(44) **penetralium**
A. inner room B. hallway C. central courtyard D. ornamental garden

(45) **aits**
A. watermeadows B. small islands C. insignificant quantities D. oaths

(46) **peons**
A. heathens B. Spanish American journeyman C. female peacocks D. hymns of praise

(47) **noils**
A. traps B. troubles C. wool-combings D. fence-posts

(48) **ruches**
A. lace frills B. disagreements C. ornaments D. cockroaches

(49) **swale**
A. loose stones B. cattle C. marshy depression D. mountain waterfall

(50) **eleemosynary**
A. worthy of imitation B. incurable C. basic D. charitable

Words from foreign languages

No language can exist or develop in complete isolation. This is more than ever true today when cultural exchange between most countries in the world has reached an unprecedented level. A few centuries ago only a highly educated élite would have known the sort of details of political, intellectual and artistic life outside their own country which are now virtually common knowledge. The extraordinary developments in communications which have been taking place since the nineteenth century have indeed made it a small world.

Of course, vast numbers of words in the English language are derived from roots in such languages as French and Latin. A book far longer than this one would be required in order to chart the various sources from which the English language is drawn and the different cultural and linguistic forces which have influenced its development into the language we know today. But there are also a number of words and phrases which have been imported wholesale into English and, although many of these are in common usage, they are still frequently misused or misunderstood.

Everyone knows what a menu is, and there can be few people who would have difficulty defining yoga, après-ski or libido (though these words have only recently become widely known). It may not be generally known that 'anorak' was originally an Eskimo word, or that 'sauna' is a direct import from Finnish, but everybody knows what the words, as adopted into English, refer to.

But saunas and anoraks are specific objects which we have assimilated into our way of life from other countries, and whose names, for convenience, we have imported with them. The words with which we are concerned in the test which follows, on the other hand, are rather more abstract than steam baths or furlined hooded coats. They are, on the whole, words which represent ideas, and which are often difficult to define precisely because they have been adopted into English to fill a gap, to express a concept for which the

English language does not have so apt a word.

This is the case, for example, with many words borrowed from German. The German language is rich in compound nouns – words made up of a number of smaller words strung together – and these often encapsulate ideas which would need a whole phrase or even, as many dictionary definitions of such words show, a whole sentence in English.

Words such as these are immensely useful and are a valuable addition to any language. All the words in the test which follows are in common use. How many of them do you know? Perhaps doing this test may help you not only to avoid making *faux pas* in your own use of words borrowed from other languages, but also to find more easily that ever-elusive *mot juste*.

As in the two preceding tests, each word is followed by four definitions, only one of which is the correct one. Make a note of the letter which corresponds to what you think is the right definition in each case and, when you have finished the whole test, check your answers with those given on page 117.

---

(1) **à la mode**
A. in fashion B. on the way C. up in arms D. at the moment

(2) **bona fide**
A. guarantee B. beware C. one who takes another's place D. genuine

(3) **per se**
A. that is B. for example C. in itself D. among other things

(4) **dénouement**
A. friendship between nations B. outcome C. confusion D. stylishness

(5) **au fait**
A. conversant B. in fact C. excepting D. out of date

(6) **ipso facto**
A. intrinsically B. under the present circumstances C. roughly speaking D. all things considered

(7) **cache**
A. hiding place B. resistance movement C. deduction from earnings D. discovery

71

(8) **bonhomie**
A. godliness B. worldly goods C. good nature D. craftiness

(9) **carte blanche**
A. the latest fashion B. menu C. sudden blow D. complete freedom

(10) **ennui**
A. soul-searching B. great pleasure C. boredom D. annoyance

(11) **milieu**
A. interim measure B. environment C. morality D. profession

(12) **putsch**
A. insurrection B. bad art C. act of senseless violence D. small dog

(13) **peccadillo**
A. downfall B. trifling offence C. small quantity D. printer's error

(14) **éclat**
A. explosion B. sudden attack C. applause D. brilliance

(15) **ambiance**
A. contentment B. surroundings C. friendliness D. balanced outlook

(16) **angst**
A. weariness B. uncertainty C. anxiety D. enlightenment

(17) **jeu d'esprit**
A. witticism B. conflict of wills C. fountain D. act of treachery

(18) **kudos**
A. hatred B. glory C. wealth D. resignation

(19) **persona non grata**
A. character in a play B. person in disguise C. unworldly person D. unacceptable person

(20) **de rigueur**
A. exhausting B. obligatory C. causing hardship D. impossible

(21) **sine qua non**
A. indispensable precondition B. bonus C. unnecessary qualification D. second to none

(22) **rapprochement**
A. arrival B. re-establishment of friendly relations C. minor disagreement D. impatience

(23) **tranche**
A. current of opinion B. club C. portion D. repayment of debt

(24) **volte face**
A. shock B. reversal of opinion C. shameless person D. break in negotiations

(25) **ex cathedra**
A. out of bounds B. lapsed churchgoer C. with religious zeal D. authoritative

(26) **contretemps**
A. argument B. unexpected mishap C. disagreement D. clumsiness

(27) **kitsch**
A. self-conscious vulgarity B. foolish person C. revolution D. subculture

(28) **mêlée**
A. mixture B. recital C. crowd of people D. brawl

(29) **nemesis**
A. nothingness B. retribution C. anonymity D. unconsciousness

(30) **cognoscenti**
A. conscientious objectors B. wine tasters C. experts D. literary men

(31) **éminence grise**
A. disreputable person B. bad influence C. the light of dawn D. the power behind the throne

(32) **parvenu**
A. upstart B. in bad taste C. renegade D. forbidden

(33) **wanderlust**
A. sexual passion B. fear of open spaces C. inexplicable yearning D. urge to travel

(34) **cachet**
A. hiding place B. prestige C. junior officer D. detachment of troops

(35) **coterie**
A. select social circle B. cut of meat C. silliness D. extravagance

(36) **demi-monde**
A. out of place B. between the wars C. people of questionable reputation D. stupid

(37) **quid pro quo**
A. existing state of affairs B. each man for himself
C. compensation for a concession D. something for nothing

(39) **leitmotif**
A. guardian angel B. recurrent theme C. bribe D. ulterior
motive

(39) **memento mori**
A. souvenir B. maternal love C. reminder of death D. confused
state of affairs

(40) **sobriquet**
A. cocktail B. bandage to stop bleeding C. floral display
D. nickname

(41) **stasis**
A. stagnation B. highest point C. boredom D. transformation

(42) **aficionado**
A. servile person B. presiding officer C. devotee D. affected
person

(43) **vade-mecum**
A. religious vow B. guidebook C. comforting illusion D. until
further notice

(44) **Gestalt**
A. secret police B. totality C. worry D. sudden understanding

(45) **chutzpah**
A. servant B. armed uprising C. contempt D. impudence

(46) **morbidezza**
A. extreme delicacy in painting B. extravagant entertainment
C. depression D. excessive fear of dying

(47) **hidalgo**
A. adventurer B. nobleman C. ruthless politician D. devil-may-
care artist

(48) **Zeitgeist**
A. spirit of the times B. sympathy C. learned politician
D. mischievous ghost

(49) **Weltanschauung**
A. cruelty B. cunning C. philosophy of life D. global crisis

(50) **Schadenfreude**
A. unfaithfulness B. misplaced affection C. enjoyment of others'
misfortunes D. deep depression

Words similar in form but different in meaning

'Comparisons are odorous' declares Constable Dogberry in Shakespeare's *Much Ado About Nothing,* and he goes on to talk about 'perjury' when he means 'perfidy' and 'burglary' when he means 'bribery'. People's misuse of words has been the subject of comedy for centuries. Indeed, it is from the name of a literary character, Mrs Malaprop (who, in Sheridan's play *The Rivals,* reveals an even wider range of verbal blind spots than Constable Dogberry), that the modern term malapropism, meaning a ludicrous misuse of a word, is derived.

Amusing though such confusions can be, they can also be very embarrassing if it is you who make them. Only recently, at a somewhat sedate dinner party, a former English student was heard to remark that a certain Russian dissident had just 'defecated to the West', which, though it livened up the party, did little to help the composure of the guest in question.

The English language is full of words which, sometimes because they derive from the same root and sometimes quite by chance, look or sound very similar to one another but have different meanings. In the case of words derived from the same root the difference in meaning may be quite subtle, but in other cases there will obviously be little or no correlation between the meanings of words which may, from their appearance, suggest a close relationship.

In the test which follows you are presented with a series of pairs of words which look or sound very similar but which mean different things. Below each pair there is a list of five definitions from which you must pick the two correct definitions for the pair of words concerned. Before you begin the test, look at the example given below. Which of the five numbered words mean the same as words A and B?

Example:

A. **bought** B. **brought**
1. sold 2. conveyed by carrying 3. took 4. purchased 5. removed

Answer:

A4 B2

Now try the two practice questions below:

(1) A. **confer** B. **concur**
1. join 2. refer 3. agree 4. disagree 5. consult

(2) A. **horde** B. **hoard**
1. goad 2. amass 3. gang 4. board 5. steal

The answers to the above questions are (1) A5 B3 and (2) A3 B2. You are now ready to go on to the test itself. When you have finished, check your answers with those given on page 118.

---

(1) A. **definite** B. **definitive**
1. final 2. uncertain 3. conditional 4. certain 5. comprehensive

(2) A. **principle** B. **principal**
1. general law 2. provincial 3. chief 4. important 5. guide

(3) A. **eligible** B. **illegible**
1. faded 2. suitable 3. educated 4. unqualified 5. unreadable

(4) A. **persecute** B. **prosecute**
1. attack 2. institute legal proceedings against 3. prohibit 4. lay down the law 5. harass

(5) A. **casual** B. **causal**
1. resultant 2. acting as a cause 3. given to adopting causes 4. unmethodical 5. highly toxic

(6) A. **fragrant** B. **flagrant**
1. wandering 2. aromatic 3. scandalous 4. unchannelled 5. carefree

(7) A. **illegitimate** B. **illiterate**
1. unassimilated 2. unable to read or write 3. criminal 4. unreadable 5. unlawful

(8) A. **allusion** B. **illusion**
1. conspiracy 2. reference 3. delusion 4. footnote 5. adherence

77

(9) A. **eclipse** B. **ellipse**
   1. outshine 2. moon 3. circle 4. oval 5. sunspot

(10) A. **adverse** B. **averse**
   1. disinclined 2. awkward 3. reverse 4. hostile 5. perverse

(11) A. **elicit** B. **illicit**
   1. select 2. draw out 3. illegal 4. solicit 5. forbid

(12) A. **affect** B. **effect**
   1. damage 2. bring about 3. result in 4. have effect on 5. fault

(13) A. **fatality** B. **fatalism**
   1. injury 2. submission to the inevitable 3. death 4. nihilism
   5. boredom

(14) A. **stationery** B. **stationary**
   1. motionless 2. cargo 3. writing materials 4. obligatory
   5. office work

(15) A. **heckle** B. **haggle**
   1. interrupt speaker with abuse 2. irritate 3. peddle 4. bargain
   5. bone of contention

(16) A. **itinerant** B. **itinerary**
   1. vagabond 2. secondary 3. irritating 4. travelling 5. route

(17) A. **sedentary** B. **sedimentary**
   1. formed by settling matter 2. routine 3. sitting 4. granular
   5. self-evident

(18) A. **officious** B. **official**
   1. meddlesome 2. diplomatic 3. offhand 4. helpful 5. authorized

(19) A. **tortuous** B. **torturous**
   1. winding 2. wrongful 3. agonizing 4. slow 5. painless

(20) A. **imitation** B. **intimation**
   1. intimacy 2. fear 3. replica 4. retribution 5. hint

(21) A. **congenial** B. **congenital**
   1. agreeable 2. reproductive 3. unpleasant 4. existing since birth
   5. incurable

(22) A. **hypocritical** B. **hypercritical**
   1. uncritical 2. crucial 3. overcritical 4. dissembling 5. medical

(23) A. **beneficent** B. **beneficial**
   1. blessed 2. advantageous 3. ecclesiastical 4. kind 5. magnificent

(24) A. **inimitable** B. **illimitable**
1. spiteful 2. unique 3. unarguable 4. limited 5. limitless

(25) A. **illusive** B. **elusive**
1. deceptive 2. suggestive 3. uncapturable 4. snobbish 5. scattering light

(26) A. **inveterate** B. **invertebrate**
1. unestablished 2. spineless 3. inaugurated 4. restless 5. habitual

(27) A. **imperious** B. **impervious**
1. royal 2. overbearing 3. porous 4. unresponsive 5. blasphemous

(28) A. **inevitably** B. **invariably**
1. probably 2. always 3. sometimes 4. never 5. unavoidably

(29) A. **dependent** B. **dependant**
1. childish 2. suspended 3. trusting 4. one who relies upon another 5. reliant

(30) A. **factitious** B. **fictitious**
1. factual 2. imaginary 3. fastidious 4. quarrelsome 5. artificial

(31) A. **momently** B. **momentarily**
1. immediately 2. presently 3. for a moment 4. from moment to moment 5. after a moment

(32) A. **climatic** B. **climactic**
1. changeable 2. weathered 3. crucial 4. culminating 5. of the weather

(33) A. **forego** B. **forgo**
1. precede 2. walk behind 3. go without 4. predict 5. preclude

(34) A. **equable** B. **equitable**
1. lawless 2. fair 3. even-tempered 4. horselike 5. innocent

(35) A. **bathos** B. **pathos**
1. anticlimax 2. sublimity 3. love 4. sadness 5. ugliness

(36) A. **emaciated** B. **emasculated**
1. made worse 2. weakened 3. thin 4. exasperated 5. destroyed

(37) A. **meretricious** B. **meritorious**
1. valuable 2. worthless 3. clever 4. falsely attractive 5. deserving praise

(38) A. **complement** B. **compliment**
1. full number 2. expression of distaste 3. implement 4. remainder 5. expression of praise

79

(39) A. **ascetic** B. **aesthetic**
1. sharp 2. appreciative of the beautiful 3. dandified 4. rendering senseless 5. self-denying

(40) A. **mendicant** B. **mendacious**
1. greedy 2. soothing 3. nomadic 4. lying 5. begging

(41) A. **obtuse** B. **abstruse**
1. acute 2. difficult to understand 3. stupid 4. obstinate 5. scattered

(42) A. **prescribe** B. **proscribe**
1. foretell 2. write down 3. terminate 4. make illegal 5. order

(43) A. **appraise** B. **apprise**
1. notify 2. laud 3. evaluate 4. lever open 5. grasp

(44) A. **holocaust** B. **hypocaust**
1. explosion 2. under-floor heating system 3. plague 4. destruction by fire 5. natural subterranean chamber

(45) A. **gregarious** B. **egregious**
1. antisocial 2. shocking 3. obsequious 4. grudging 5. sociable

(46) A. **ingenuous** B. **ingenious**
1. artistic 2. artless 3. strange 4. cleverly contrived 5. evil

(47) A. **invidious** B. **insidious**
1. troublesome 2. proceeding by stealth 3. offensive 4. tyrannical 5. baleful

(48) A. **torrid** B. **torpid**
1. sluggish 2. humid 3. lascivious 4. missile 5. hot

(49) A. **immanent** B. **imminent**
1. overbearing 2. impending 3. primary 4. inherent 5. transcendent

(50) A. **ordinance** B. **ordnance**
1. map 2. cardinal 3. cannon 4. rising tract of land 5. decree

Words with more than one meaning

One wonders how many people have knocked themselves half-unconscious before realizing the meaning of the sign DUCK OR GROUSE which is to be seen over so many low doorways or ceiling beams in old houses. Words like these, which are identical in form but have more than one meaning, are called homonyms, and their derivations often provide interesting insights into the way in which language develops. For example, the two meanings of the word 'duck' which are played upon in the warning sign mentioned above would seem to be drawn from the same root, the Old English word *dūcan* meaning 'to dive'. The connection between ducks and diving needs no elaboration. The two meanings of the word 'grouse', on the other hand, derive from completely different sources. The wild bird was given its name in the sixteenth century, probably from the Welsh word *grugiar* (*grug* meaning 'heath' and *iar* meaning 'hen'). The origin of the word 'grouse' meaning 'grumble' is, however, still a mystery, although the word seems not to have been used before the nineteenth century.

Homonyms provide good examples of the opportunities for both misunderstanding and enrichment of meaning which language continually presents. At one end of the scale there is the simple *double entendre,* the double meaning, with which every schoolboy is familiar. One has only to listen to television comedy shows to see how easily apparently innocent comments can be given less innocent meanings if their context is manipulated. At the other end of the scale, writers as far removed as Shakespeare and Dylan Thomas have demonstrated a fascination with the interplay of sound and meaning which, when all's said, constitutes the basis of language itself, and reminds us, as sometimes we tend to forget, that words are there both to be used and to be enjoyed.

In the test which follows you are presented with a series of pairs of definitions and you must find a word to which both definitions apply.

81

Work through the test as quickly as you can, but before you start, look at the example given below.

Example:

    (1) A. miserly
           B. intend   _____

Answer:

    mean

When you have finished as much of the test as you can, check your answers with those given on page 118.

---

(1) A. remainder
      B. repose

(2) A. solid and reliable
      B. noise

(3) A. riverside
      B. depository for money

(4) A. rear of ship
      B. austere

(5) A. gift
      B. the time now passing

(6) A. portray
      B. pull out

(7) A. of high quality
      B. money paid for an offence

(8) A. forefront of army
      B. light vehicle

(9) A. shut
      B. near

(10) A. solemn
       B. excavation for burial

(11) A. fireplace
B. shred against rough surface   _____

(12) A. single-masted fishing boat
B. slap   _____

(13) A. try to win the favour of
B. space enclosed by walls or buildings   _____

(14) A. perpendicular headland
B. deceive by pretence of strength   _____

(15) A. shouts or jeers at performers
B. soldiers' lodgings   _____

(16) A. hurry
B. waterside plant   _____

(17) A. violent concussion
B. shaggy mass of hair   _____

(18) A. intended prey
B. place where stone is excavated   _____

(19) A. soft
B. offer   _____

(20) A. postal marking
B. open and honest   _____

(21) A. old saying
B. observed   _____

(22) A. rub off part of skin
B. feed on growing grass   _____

(23) A. type of flatfish
B. struggle in water   _____

(24) A. total
B. speak   _____

(25) A. compress lips
B. money bag   _____

(26) A. strike discordant note
B. spoutless earthenware etc vessel   _____

(27) A. type of firearm
B. search and rob   _____

(28) A. practise swordplay
     B. receiver of stolen goods   _____

(29) A. alleviation of distress
     B. raised design   _____

(30) A. lose one's vigour
     B. bunting attached to pole as ensign   _____

(31) A. offspring
     B. sulk   _____

(32) A. acrobat
     B. type of drinking glass   _____

(33) A. tension
     B. snatch of music   _____

(34) A. foliage
     B. departs   _____

(35) A. seashore
     B. ride down hill etc without using power   _____

(36) A. ill humour
     B. make a fuss of   _____

(37) A. fungoid growth
     B. give shape to   _____

(38) A. one incapacitated by illness
     B. having no legal force   _____

(39) A. catch sight of
     B. episcopal unit   _____

(40) A. boundary fence
     B. faintly coloured   _____

(41) A. wind-blown water droplets
     B. sprig of flowers   _____

(42) A. explanation of text
     B. superficial shine   _____

(43) A. woman's silk wrap
     B. purloined   _____

(44) A. mars
     B. plunder   _____

(45) A. cut
B. uninspired writer   _____

(46) A. long-necked vessel for distilling liquids
B. reply   _____

(47) A. material thing
B. express disapproval   _____

(48) A. land mass
B. chaste   _____

(49) A. cast a spell over
B. way in   _____

(50) A. capable of being fertilized
B. proof against attack   _____

Homophones

Words which sound similar to one another but which have different meanings are known as homophones. The title of *Just Desserts*, a cookbook, contains both a homonym and a homophone. 'Just' is a homonym – it means both 'fair' (in the cliché 'just deserts') and 'nothing other than' in the book title. 'Desserts', on the other hand, is a homophone – spelt as it is in the book title it obviously refers to the course which follows the main course of a meal, while spelt 'deserts' in the phrase on which the author is punning, it means 'deservings'.

Homophones are often used as puns, even in the most serious literature. In Shakespeare's tragedy *Macbeth*, just after Macbeth has murdered the sleeping Duncan, Lady Macbeth takes the bloody daggers from her husband and goes back into Duncan's bedchamber in order to frame the murdered man's attendants. As she goes she says:

> If he do bleed,
> I'll gild the faces of the grooms withal,
> For it must seem their guilt.

The word 'guilt' here is a homophone of 'gilt' (meaning a thin layer of gold), the pun following on from the use of the word 'gild' in the previous line.

In the test which follows you are presented with a series of pairs of meanings. Each pair defines two words which sound alike. It is up to you to find the words in question. Before you begin the test, look at the example given below.

Example:

(1) A. change the characteristics of   _____
    B. communion table in church   _____

Answer:

    A. alter
    B. altar

Work through the test as quickly as you can. When you have done as much of it as you can, check your answers with those given on page 119.

---

(1) A. impregnate with colouring matter   _____

      B. expire   _____

(2) A. street   _____

      B. travelled on horseback   _____

(3) A. quietude   _____

      B. section of a whole   _____

(4) A. conceited   _____

      B. blood vessel   _____

(5) A. coarse in texture   _____

      B. elaborate starched collar with lace frills   _____

(6) A. long-drawn-out cry of complaint   _____

      B. fermented grape juice   _____

(7) A. main branch of a tree   _____

      B. bend as a sign of respect   _____

(8) A. long breaths drawn out of sadness   _____

      B. magnitude   _____

(9) A. steps between adjacent fields   _____

      B. manner of writing or speaking   _____

(10) A. just and unbiased   _____

      B. price paid by passenger   _____

(11) A. put to death   _____

     B. toboggan   _____

(12) A. ale   _____

     B. frame on which coffin is placed   _____

(13) A. lowest male vocal range   _____

     B. morally despicable   _____

(14) A. apprehended   _____

     B. plot of ground on which tennis is played   _____

(15) A. monetary gain   _____

     B. seer   _____

(16) A. instructed   _____

     B. not slack   _____

(17) A. sacred   _____

     B. entirely   _____

(18) A. rogue   _____

     B. main body of church   _____

(19) A. unadorned   _____

     B. level surface   _____

(20) A. pointed summit of mountain   _____

     B. ill-feeling   _____

(21) A. estimated without detailed calculation   _____

     B. person visiting another   _____

(22) A. permitted   _____

     B. audibly   _____

(23) A. inquired impertinently   _____

     B. haughtiness   _____

(24) A. young swan   _____

     B. ring with seal set into it   _____

(25) A. brass plate used as percussion
instrument   _____

B. mark or object taken to represent
something else   _____

(26) A. pure   _____

B. pursued   _____

(27) A. vision   _____

B. quote as authority   _____

(28) A. poet   _____

B. prohibited   _____

(29) A. more audacious   _____

B. large weather-worn stone   _____

(30) A. plait   _____

B. made a donkey-like sound   _____

(31) A. concocts   _____

B. contusion   _____

(32) A. atmospheric conditions   _____

B. castrated ram   _____

(33) A. grey-haired with age   _____

B. prostitute   _____

(34) A. deep ditch surrounding
house or castle   _____

B. particle of dust   _____

(35) A. anger   _____

B. neckband of shirt   _____

(36) A. thickly inhabited   _____

B. the common people   _____

(37) A. makes a further remark   _____

B. cutting tool with long curved blade _____

89

(38) A. make hostile inroads into
     another country   _____

    B. spoke violently   _____

(39) A. play games of chance for money   _____

    B. caper   _____

(40) A. lift   _____

    B. level with the ground by complete
     destruction   _____

(41) A. horrible and terrifying   _____

    B. greyish   _____

(42) A. swoon   _____

    B. sham attack to divert opponent's
     attention   _____

(43) A. unobtrusive   _____

    B. individually distinct   _____

(44) A. embankment against river floods   _____

    B. impose tax etc   _____

(45) A. tool for boring holes   _____

    B. foretell   _____

(46) A. strong unbleached cloth used in
     painting   _____

    B. solicit votes from   _____

(47) A. watery discharge or catarrh   _____

    B. space   _____

(48) A. spirit distilled from grain and
     flavoured with juniper berries   _____

    B. Muslim spirits with supernatural
     power over mankind   _____

(49) A. young deer   _____

    B. rural deity with horns and tail   _____

(50) A. bell rung as an alarm signal   _____

    B. poison of animal or vegetable origin   _____

Synonyms

A synonym is a word which either is identical in sense to another word or has the same general sense as another word but is perhaps appropriate to a different context. How often have you found yourself asking 'What's another word for . . . ?' and coming up with various alternatives, all of which almost, but not completely, fit the bill? So near and yet so far. Or, perhaps, so close and yet so distant.

In the test which follows, every question presents you with two words. You have to find a third word which means the same as the first word and rhymes with the second. Before you begin the test, look at the example given below.

Example:

(1) tie   ——————————   signed

Answer:

bind

Set yourself a time limit of 12 minutes in which to do as much of the test as you can. Then check your answers with those given on page 120.

---

(1) kill	————————	pray
(2) fury	————————	page
(3) adoration	————————	above
(4) noisy	————————	crowd
(5) countenance	————————	case

(6) menace	————————	yet
(7) conspiracy	————————	not
(7) free	————————	peace
(9) stay	————————	train
(10) avoid	————————	paid
(11) promise	————————	hedge
(12) stem	————————	talk
(13) salute	————————	treat
(14) praise	————————	cord
(15) rotate	————————	solve
(16) cellar	————————	malt
(17) skin	————————	day
(18) boast	————————	taunt
(19) fight	————————	tall
(20) hate	————————	bore
(21) tepid	————————	storm
(22) smell	————————	peak
(23) bury	————————	refer
(24) scatter	————————	blue
(25) long	————————	turn
(26) summary	————————	racy
(27) insult	————————	guile
(28) enthusiasm	————————	curve
(29) chasm	————————	kiss
(30) obscene	————————	rude
(31) savour	————————	hellish
(32) frost	————————	time
(33) submerge	————————	reverse

(34) artless	————————	believe
(35) erroneous	————————	gracious
(36) extinguish	————————	mouse
(37) affirm	————————	deter
(38) false	————————	curious
(39) horselike	————————	malign
(40) cougar	————————	tumour
(41) suave	————————	retain
(42) corrupt	————————	initiate
(43) rail	————————	away
(44) accuse	————————	alight
(45) revenant	————————	toast
(46) sharpen	————————	tone
(47) hasty	————————	bursary
(48) fertile	————————	rotund
(49) useless	————————	comatose
(50) melt	————————	repress

6. Tests of usage and verbal reasoning

Transposition of words

It is only too easy to read what you expect to read rather than what is actually there. This is particularly true now that the pace of modern communications often makes it necessary to scan a document very quickly and to pick out the relevant sections accurately on a single reading.

Scarcely a day goes by without an advertisement for 'speed reading' courses appearing in the newspapers. Such courses are designed to help you learn to gather the gist of what you read and to alight on the most important parts without having to take in each individual word. To some extent, of course, this is what most people do anyway when they are reading, but it is in many ways a dangerous approach and can easily become counterproductive if taken to extremes. How often, for example, have you read a passage in a book or a newspaper and thought you have understood it, only to find, on a closer reading, that you have missed many of the finer points and have in fact gained a very distorted idea of the author's argument? Furthermore, the more careful the writer has been to communicate his or her meaning precisely, the more you will inevitably be missing by merely scanning the words at speed.

The following test is designed to combine swift reading with attention to detail. In each of the sentences below two words are transposed. In some of the earlier sentences the words concerned are quite easy to spot, but in the later ones they may prove a little more difficult to find. Set yourself a time limit of ten minutes in which to do as much of the test as you can. Before you start, look at the example given below.

Example:

Because it was built on a valley the house commanded a spectacular view of the hill below.

The words *valley* and *hill* must be transposed in the above sentence for it to make sense. In the test which follows you should underline the words which must be transposed. Remember that you only have ten minutes in which to finish. At the end of that time, check your answers with those given on page 120.

---

(1) John, like most mistakes, never learnt from his people.

(2) The ball rebounded off the goalkeeper and was punched out by the crossbar.

(3) He fought with the man of a strength half his age.

(4) In most serious countries this is no longer a developed problem.

(5) In the house order prevailed throughout the end.

(6) Valour is the better part of discretion.

(7) He gave a very recent account of his confusing adventures.

(8) He earns enough money to keep a family of comfort in four if not in luxury.

(9) The young man met the Count's challenge and, at four o'clock the next morning, they accepted for a duel on the heath.

(10) Volcanic eruption from the ash has been found as far north as Paris.

(11) The passengers assured the pilot that there was no cause for alarm.

(12) During heatwaves there is always the danger that countryside fires will sweep the forest.

(13) He anticipated more for the goods than he had paid.

(14) After months of relentless rain, sunshine finally fell on the parched countryside.

(15) The guide, who knew every inch of the journey, pointed out interest of places along the route.

(16) 'You can like whatever you say about Fred' said George, 'but I still don't trust him'.

(17) She added the prices together with a total conviction that the

growing would be more than she could afford.

(18) Even among those who wield extraordinary power, every few people regard their very action as important.

(19) The first two critics were well received by the performers who attended the concert.

(20) Most people who have lived through a period of upheaval have observed that the adversity spirit is strongest in community.

(21) When the people heard the sermon they saw the ways of their error.

(22) The committee discussed the time for some motion before deciding ultimately to reject it.

(23) He had a claustrophobic dread of being confined for any length of time in a trapped space.

(24) It was mainly to satisfy his own cause that he championed the conscience of the oppressed.

(25) If he had asked the question it was as when a great weight had been lifted from his mind.

(26) Paul was not a dishonest person, but nobody ever trusted him completely because he knew quite what nobody was thinking.

(27) There is often a freshness about professional music-making which the amateur, who has to make a living from giving performances, can find it difficult to achieve.

(28) It is possible that, given resources, the tribes of this particular desert may unite in the quest for encouragement.

(29) 'I thought I saw something right under that third bush on the move.'

(30) The stability of large numbers of people on a temporary basis does not make for long-term economic employment.

(31) Almost everyone who met him agreed that he remained great despite his meteoric rise to fame and his modest talent.

(32) 'Excuse my asking, but you are likely to be going down to London in the near future?'

(33) As soon as we entered the forest we felt we were in the danger of some mortal presence.

(34) Nothing you will say can convince me that murder is ever justifiable.

(35) Examples have proved that archaeologists of Roman occupation exist even in the most remote parts of the country.

(36) There was seldom little doubt in their minds that, by protesting against the demolition plans, they were doing their best to save any communities like Gonville Street from extinction.

(37) The way of life we had only dreamed about seemed suddenly of to become a possibility.

(38) There is nothing more likely to produce conflict than issues over basic policy differences.

(39) Despite the disapproval of many visitors to the country, Spain still attracts large crowds in bullfighting.

(40) Its a well-known fact that under normal conditions water will eventually find it's own level.

The right word in the right place

We all have moments when we struggle to find the right word for what we want to say. Sometimes we find it in the end; at other times it eludes us altogether. Either way, the interim is infuriating. Many words spring to mind, some of them almost right for the job, some because they sound similar to the word we have at the back of our mind, others for no apparent reason whatsoever.

In the following test you are given a number of sentences, each of which has a one-word blank to be filled in. After each sentence there are four words. One of the words will fill the blank so that the sentence makes sense. Make a note of the letter which corresponds to the correct word in each case and, when you have finished the whole test, check your answers with those given on page 121.

---

(1) The publication of this catalogue does not _____ the possibility of later alterations.

   A. include B. conclude C. preclude D. seclude

(2) His complexion was so _____ that we wondered if he was ill.

   A. pallid B. pellucid C. palliative D. palatable

(3) Despite a promising start, Atkinson's work this term has been somewhat _____.

   A. erotic B. erratic C. ecstatic D. exotic

(4) _____ hostility was the hallmark of the resistance movement until it felt strong enough to act in the open.

   A. Covert B. Overt C. Introverted D. Extroverted

(5) Jack was a _____ reader of cheap novels.

A. viscous B. vicious C. veracious D. voracious

(6) It is to be hoped that the present climatic conditions will _____ to a better harvest.

A. induce B. conduce C. produce D. reduce

(7) John's acceptance of the invitation was only _____ because he was not sure whether he was seeing Jane that evening.

A. provisional B. providential C. provincial D. proverbial

(8) 'We are devoting this period to _____ of our earlier advances.'

A. solidity B. solidification C. consolidation D. solidarity

(9) Despite the unsavoury conditions in which he lived, he remained _____ in his personal habits.

A. fatuous B. fastidious C. fallacious D. facetious

(10) The novel lacked conviction because of the _____ actions of the characters.

A. impractical B. implacable C. impeccable D. implausible

(11) His gratitude expressed itself in a _____ prayer of thanksgiving.

A. spurious B. spontaneous C. spasmodic D. sporadic

(12) He delivered a tedious _____ on the subject of financial self-sufficiency.

A. acquisition B. inquisition C. disquisition D. requisition

(13) The President's speech was mainly _____ of attacks on his predecessor's policies.

A. comprised B. composed C. consisted D. contained

(14) The drunkard was so _____ in his demands that Sir William eventually gave him a shilling in order to get rid of him.

A. improvident B. impotent C. importunate D. impolitic

(15) Alice admitted that she _____ felt exhausted by the end of week.

A. inevitably B. inveterately C. invariably D. involuntarily

(16) Only by a massive effort of _____ could he disguise his love for her.

A. dissimilation B. dissimulation C. dissipation D. dissolution

(17 The author's masterful _____ of the atmosphere of his childhood helped to make the book an overnight success.

A. evocation B. invocation C. provocation D. convocation

(18) The film was shown on two _____ nights.

A. consistent B. consecutive C. concurrent D. consequential

(19) It has often been said that the pleasures of this world are _____ compared with those of the next.

A. transient B. transitional C. transitive D. transcendental

(20) 'How can we believe this witness when no one will _____ his story?'

A. collate B. correlate C. collaborate D. corroborate

(21) Private enterprise is bound to flourish in a _____ economy.

A. budgeting B. burgeoning C. bludgeoning D. buttressing

(22) The jury's _____ was stretched to the limit by what they heard.

A. credit B. credence C. credibility D. credulity

(23) The _____ he felt towards her was so great that he could not even pass her in the street without insulting her.

A. sympathy B. empathy C. antipathy D. antiphony

(24) _____ as he was, he was taken advantage of by those more versed in the ways of the commercial world.

A. Callow B. Sallow C. Tallow D. Fallow

(25) His literary style was _____ to the point of affectation.

A. seditious B. salacious C. salubrious D. sententious

(26) The _____ of 'lascivious' is 'chaste'.

A. antonynm B. synonym C. homonym D. acronym

(27) His feelings about Adrienne remained _____ despite their long acquaintance.

A. ambient B. ambivalent C. ambidextrous D. ambiguous

(28) 'Don't _____', said the official, 'I want a decision now'.

A. prevaricate B. predicate C. perorate D. precipitate

(29) 'I shall now _____ the aspects of the question with which I shall later be dealing.'

A. abdicate B. abrogate C. abnegate D. adumbrate

(30) Few tribes are _____ to this wilderness of rocks and parched earth.

A. indigent B. indigenous C. indicative D. indolent

(31) She had an extensive collection of such _____ publications as playbills and railway timetables.

A. ephemeral B. ethereal C. empirical D. episcopal

(32) Despite their _____ dangers, the advantages of the scheme were felt to be a strong recommendation.

A. consonant B. concomitant C. concordant D. congruent

(33) His pleasure at seeing her proved _____ since he soon realized it was Frank she had come to talk to.

A. effete B. effluent C. effervescent D. evanescent

(34) The priest warned the Count that he was in danger of commiting a _____ sin.

A. venal B. venial C. venereal D. viral

101

(35) So unstinting was the speaker's _____ upon the dead man that even those who had criticized him most severely when he was alive came away wondering whether they had wronged him.

A. elegy B. eulogy C. euphony D. epiphany

(36) The strength of the Professor's argument was seriously undermined by his drawing of _____ comparisons between unrelated subjects.

A. tenable B. tenacious C. tenuous D. tendentious

(37) His unpopular views made him the subject of much _____.

A. obduracy B. obfuscation C. obloquy D. obtrusion

(38) She took the opportunity to _____ her son for his irresponsible behaviour.

A. exonerate B. exculpate C. extenuate D. excoriate

(39) His _____ studies had made him one of the country's foremost experts on dragonflies.

A. etymological B. entomological C. ornithological D. ontological

(40) The _____ surface of the standing pool was brightened only by a scattering of crimson petals from an overhanging rosebush.

A. glaucous B. gibbous C. glabrous D. glutinous

Relationships between words

'What's it like?' is a question frequently asked by people who want to form an idea of something they haven't seen or experienced. The form of the question suggests that we try to understand unfamiliar things by comparing them with other things already within our experience. In other words, the human mind works by making connections between objects and between ideas, and by placing them in relationships to one another.

Perhaps this is why so many employers use tests of verbal reasoning such as the next two tests in this book in order to assess potential employees. Part of the purpose of tests like these is to see how *quickly* you can make connections between words, so, in each of the following tests, you should set yourself a time limit in which to do as much of each test as you can.

In this first test you are presented with a series of sentences with the first word and the last word missing. You have to find the words to fill the blanks so that each sentence makes sense. For the first blank you should choose one of the numbered words and for the second blank one of the lettered ones. Make a note of the number and letter which correspond to the words you have chosen in each case.

Before you begin the test, look at the example given below.

Example:

_____ is to wrong as good is to _____

1. cruel 2. right 3. left 4. insult
A. proper B. virtue C. love D. bad

Answer:
2D

Allow yourself 12 minutes in which to do as much of the test as you can. After that time, check your answers with those given on page 121.

(1) _____ is to girl as man is to _____

    1. father 2. doll 3. boy 4. mother
    A. woman B. old C. husband D. child

(2) _____ is to end as first is to _____

    1. finish 2. beginning 3. close 4. complete
    A. incomplete B. last C. second D. third

(3) _____ is to hate as friend is to _____

    1. love 2. fight 3. dislike 4. despise
    A. like B. companion C. enemy D. trust

(4) _____ is to fish as run is to _____

    1. swim 2. ship 3. seaweed 4. water
    A. drown B. hare C. tortoise D. walk

(5) _____ is to night as light is to _____

    1. dream 2. ship 3. dark 4. bed
    A. day B. sun C. heavy D. rise

(6) _____ is to pig as beef is to _____

    1. piglet 2. pork 3. sty 4. farmyard
    A. lamb B. herd C. farmer D. bullock

(7) _____ is to pipe as pianist is to _____

    1. smoke 2. tobacco 3. piper 4. music
    A. symphony B. piano C. concert D. keys

(8) _____ is to Wales as English is to _____

    1. rugby 2. Ireland 3. border 4. Welsh
    A. language B. England C. football D. Scotland

(9) _____ is to bathroom as sleep is to _____

    1. basin 2. wash 3. soap 4. morning
    A. wake B. bed C. night D. bedroom

(10) _____ is to whisper as strike is to _____

    1. quiet 2. shout 3. anger 4. breeze
    A. touch B. noisy C. match D. kill

(11) _____ is to sorrow as strength is to _____

1. tear 2. loss 3. happiness 4. console
A. lion B. crush C. muscle D. weakness

(12) _____ are to crowd as trees are to _____

1. people 2. police 3. mobs 4. shouts
A. woodman B. forest C. shrubs D. branches

(13) _____ is to square as sphere is to _____

1. oblong 2. cube 3. sugar 4. polygon
A. cylinder B. world C. circle D. segment

(14) _____ is to air as boat is to _____

1. fly 2. oxygen 3. breathe 4. aeroplane
A. ship B. float C. water D. harbour

(15) _____ is to whisky as brew is to _____

1. rye 2. distil 3. spirit 4. gin
A. sugar B. hops C. ferment D. beer

(16) _____ is to composer as fresco is to _____

1. Beethoven 2. orchestra 3. symphony 4. piano
A. chapel B. Leonardo C. painter D. colours

(17) _____ is to time as speedometer is to _____

1. clock 2. day 3. minute 4. year
A. car B. road C. velocity D. miles

(18) _____ is to kill as serpent is to _____

1. revive 2. slay 3. murderer 4. knife
A. snake B. Eden C. lizard D. wriggle

(19) _____ is to fruit as carrot is to _____

1. tree 2. orchard 3. apple 4. bowl
A. potato B. stew C. vegetable D. pear

(20) _____ is to breadth as strong is to _____

1. square 2. length 3. deep 4. broad
A. strength B. weak C. powerful D. short

(21) _____ is to woman as cub is to _____

　　1. man 2. wife 3. baby 4. home
　　A. boy B. vixen C. lair D. birth

(22) _____ is to poor as wealth is to _____

　　1. pauper 2. poverty 3. cold 4. rich
　　A. wealthy B. money C. miser D. fortune

(23) _____ is to leg as stammer is to _____

　　1. foot 2. run 3. knee 4. limp
　　A. stutter B. shout C. voice D. hesitate

(24) _____ is to elude as arrest is to _____

　　1. criminal 2. escape 3. confuse 4. prison
　　A. policeman B. crime C. capture D. free

(25) _____ is to sew as sword is to _____

　　1. skirt 2. needle 3. hem 4. stitch
　　A. fence B. sharp C. blade D. dagger

(26) _____ is to pupils as priest is to _____

　　1. lesson 2. school 3. teacher 4. homework
　　A. church B. congregation C. God D. sermon

(27) _____ is to hurricane as pond is to _____

　　1. rain 2. breeze 3. blow 4. winter
　　A. ocean B. deep C. puddle D. water

(28) _____ is to irascible as haughty is to _____

　　1. proud 2. strange 3. sorry 4. phlegmatic
　　A. peacock B. overbearing C. kind D. humble

(29) _____ is to colour as deaf is to _____

　　1. blue 2. paint 3. blind 4. see
　　A. tone B. hear C. dumb D. noisy

(30) _____ is to cutlery as plate is to _____

　　1. axe 2. knife 3. butcher 4. kitchen
　　A. cup B. crockery C. saucer D. glass

106

(31) _____ is to egg as plant is to _____

    1. chicken 2. yolk 3. boil 4. shell
    A. garden B. earth C. seed D. flower

(32) _____ is to cooking as thespian is to _____

    1. ingredient 2. food 3. culinary 4. kitchen
    A. writing B. acting C. Greek D. ancient

(33) _____ is to hill as crest is to _____

    1. climb 2. summit 3. mole 4. river
    A. mountain B. top C. wave D. descend

(34) _____ is to all as few is to _____

    1. none 2. most 3. each 4. more
    A. less B. many C. nothing D. some

(35) _____ is to tree as silk is to _____

    1. leaf 2. forest 3. axe 4. rubber
    A. worm B. lace C. nightgown D. flower

(36) _____ is to destroy as mend is to _____

    1. make 2. use 3. builder 4. plague
    A. repair B. improve C. replace D. damage

(37) _____ is to hearing as television is to _____

    1. ear 2. deaf 3. radio 4. cinema
    A. blindness B. eye C. sight D. programme

(38) _____ is to gavel as conductor is to _____

    1. labourer 2. banker 3. money 4. auctioneer
    A. violin B. baton C. music D. orchestra

(39) _____is to fly as bird is to _____

    1. bee 2. insect 3. walk 4. swim
    A. sparrow B. nest C. seed D. wing

(40) _____ is to opera as poem is to _____

1. actor 2. play 3. hero 4. tune
A. poet B. piano C. song D. words

Odd ones out

This next test is also a test of relationships between words, and you should set yourself a time limit of ten minutes in which to do as much of it as you can.

In each of the questions which follow you are given six words. Four of the words are related to one another in some way. The other two are odd ones out. It is up to you to spot the odd ones out and to make a note of the letters which correspond to the words concerned.

Before you begin the test, look at the example given below.

Example:

A. man B. father C. girl D. husband E. wife F. uncle

Answer:

C E

Girl and *wife* are the odd ones out because all the rest are male. Remember that you have only ten minutes in which to do as much of the test as you can. When the time is up, check your answers with those given on page 122.

---

(1) A. horse B. stable C. cow D. pig E. sheep F. barn

(2) A. Spanish B. Welsh C. Holland D. German E. French F. England

(3) A. aeroplane B. balloon C. yacht D. steamer E. liner F. catamaran

(4) A. flute B. piano C. conductor D. oboe E. baton F. violin

(5) A. fast B. slow C. speedy D. ponderous E. swift F. quick

(6) A. open B. closed C. shut D. lock E. ajar F. hinge

(7) A. mountain B. hill C. river D. valley E. stream F. heath

(8) A. clock B. year C. minute D. month E. calendar F. day

(9) A. gin B. whisky C. coffee D. brandy E. port F. tea

(10) A. callous B. cruel C. heartless D. benign E. malevolent F. thoughtful

(11) A. chair B. wall C. ceiling D. table E. roof F. floor

(12) A. oak B. iron C. tin D. lead E. ebony F. copper

(13) A. much B. many C. more D. fewer E. none F. some

(14) A. doctor B. Frenchman C. musician D. tribesman E. sailor F. publisher

(15) A. Anglican B. Christian C. Muslim D. Jew E. Hindu F. Baptist

(16) A. heart B. soul C. lung D. kidney E. liver F. mind

(17) A. mourn B. lament C. bewail D. remember E. keen F. celebrate

(18) A. Asia B. France C. Canada D. Australia E. Africa F. Europe

(19) A. drive B. veer C. swerve D. reverse E. turn F. accelerate

(20) A. second B. two C. double D. bipartite E. one F. four

(21) A. house B. village C. town D. wigwam E. igloo F. cottage

(22) A. mosque B. church C. chapel D. hall E. synagogue F. mansion

(23) A. crime B. police C. army D. murder E. riot squad F. guard

(24) A. juggernaut B. pantechnicon C. car D. van E. limousine F. taxi

(25) A. sincere B. hypocritical C. honest D. deceitful E. affected F. lying

(26) A. mercury B. neon C. methane D. oxygen E. hydrogen F. sulphur

(27) A. open B. overt C. surreptitious D. clandestine E. covert F. hidden

(28) A. overrun B. conquer C. retreat D. gain E. lose F. annex

(29) A. transitory B. intractable C. fundamental D. solid
      E. permanent F. temporary

(30) A. Pluto B. Sirius C. Mars D. Orion E. Saturn F. Jupiter

(31) A. square B. circle C. cube D. parallelogram E. cylinder
      F. ellipse

(32) A. conflict B. skirmish C. truce D. battle E. war F. armistice

(33) A. cat B. lion C. wolf D. lynx E. hyena F. puma

(34) A. see B. understand C. touch D. taste E. smell F. suspect

(35) A. commute B. mitigate C. intensify D. reduce E. alleviate
      F. escalate

(36) A. marionette B. pierrot C. puppet D. harlequin E. clown
      F. troubadour

(37) A. vault B. cellar C. chapel D. chamber E. basement
      F. oubliette

(38) A. violin B. clarinet C. cello D. double bass E. viola
      F. bassoon

(39) A. surprise B. astonish C. amaze D. wonder E. astound
      F. marvel

(40) A. actual B. insubstantial C. shadowy D. illusory E. ethereal
      F. existent

PART THREE:
ANSWERS TO THE TESTS

Spelling tests

Words out of context

(1) A	(14) A	(27) A	(40) A
(2) A	(15) A	(28) A	(41) A
(3) B	(16) B	(29) A	(42) B
(4) A	(17) A	(30) A	(43) A
(5) B	(18) B	(31) B	(44) B
(6) A	(19) A	(32) A	(45) B
(7) B	(20) A	(33) B	(46) A
(8) B	(21) A	(34) B	(47) A
(9) A	(22) A	(35) A	(48) B
(10) B	(23) A	(36) B	(49) A
(11) B	(24) B	(37) A	(50) A
(12) A	(25) A	(38) B	
(13) B	(26) B	(39) A	

Words in context

(1) gorilla
(2) fortieth
(3) hindrance
(4) exaggeration
(5) flagons
(6) aberration
(7) led
(8) lath
(9) knowledgeable
(10) obsequiousness
(11) unravelled
(12) veterinary
(13) pomegranates
(14) gaiety
(15) underrated
(16) smooth
(17) ferreting
(18) kleptomania
(19) gist
(20) chilblains
(21) harebrained
(22) sacrilegious
(23) meanness
(24) lightning
(25) guinea-pig
(26) filament

115

(27) gruesome
(28) forgo
(29) heroin
(30) pavilion
(31) fictitious
(32) allotment
(33) idyllic

(34) volcanoes
(35) intractable
(36) sanguine
(37) recompense
(38) racquets
(39) idiosyncrasy
(40) diarrhoea

Definition tests

Words from the news

(1) A	(14) C	(27) B	(40) C
(2) C	(15) A	(28) D	(41) B
(3) C	(16) B	(29) C	(42) D
(4) B	(17) D	(30) D	(43) B
(5) A	(18) C	(31) C	(44) B
(6) D	(19) C	(32) B	(45) D
(7) B	(20) B	(33) B	(46) A
(8) A	(21) B	(34) A	(47) A
(9) B	(22) A	(35) B	(48) A
(10) B	(23) B	(36) C	(49) D
(11) A	(24) B	(37) D	(50) B
(12) D	(25) A	(38) C	
(13) B	(26) C	(39) A	

Words from works of literature

(1) D (*Herzog*, Saul Bellow)
(2) B (*Nineteen Eighty-four*, George Orwell)
(3) B (*Decline and Fall*, Evelyn Waugh)
(4) A (*Robinson Crusoe*, Daniel Defoe)
(5) B (*Maiden Castle*, John Cowper Powys)
(6) D (*The Adventures of Peregrine Pickle*, Tobias Smollett)
(7) A (*Corridors of Power*, C P Snow)
(8) A (*The Man of Property*, John Galsworthy)
(9) C (*The Great Gatsby*, F Scott Fitzgerald)
(10) B (*North and South*, Elizabeth Gaskell)
(11) A (*Of Human Bondage*, W Somerset Maugham)
(12) C (*Erewhon*, Samuel Butler)
(13) A (*The Moonstone*, Wilkie Collins)

(14) B (*A Fairy Tale of New York*, J P Donleavy)
(15) C (*The Return of the Native*, Thomas Hardy)
(16) D (*The Portrait of a Lady*, Henry James)
(17) A (*Bech: a Book*, John Updike)
(18) C (*Moby Dick*, Herman Melville)
(19) A (*The War of the Worlds*, H G Wells)
(20) D (*Gormenghast*, Mervyn Peake)
(21) C (*Nightmare Abbey*, Thomas Peacock)
(22) A (*A Passage to India*, E M Forster)
(23) B (*Vanity Fair*, William Makepeace Thackeray)
(24) D (*Jane Eyre*, Charlotte Brontë)
(25) B (*The Hound of the Baskervilles*, Arthur Conan Doyle)
(26) C (*The Unvanquished*, William Faulkner)
(27) C (*Catch 22*, Joseph Heller)
(28) D (*Justine*, Lawrence Durrell)
(29) A (*The Life of Samuel Johnson*, James Boswell)
(30) B (*Ulysses*, James Joyce)
(31) C (*Daniel Martin*, John Fowles)
(32) C (*Old Mortality*, Sir Walter Scott)
(33) C (*Jacob's Room*, Virginia Woolf)
(34) C (*Anna of the Five Towns*, Arnold Bennett)
(35) B (*Sense and Sensibility*, Jane Austen)
(36) B (*Brave New World*, Aldous Huxley)
(37) B (*Middlemarch*, George Eliot)
(38) D (*The Scarlet Letter*, Nathaniel Hawthorne)
(39) C (*The Eustace Diamonds*, Anthony Trollope)
(40) B (*The Picture of Dorian Gray*, Oscar Wilde)
(41) B (*The Life and Opinions of Tristram Shandy*, Laurence Sterne)
(42) D (*The Inimitable Jeeves*, P G Wodehouse)
(43) C (*A Burnt-out Case*, Graham Greene)
(44) A (*Wuthering Heights*, Emily Brontë)
(45) B (*Bleak House*, Charles Dickens)
(46) B (*Nostromo*, Joseph Conrad)
(47) C (*The Good Companions*, J B Priestley)
(48) A (*Women in Love*, D H Lawrence)
(49) C (*East of Eden*, John Steinbeck)
(50) D (*Tom Jones*, Henry Fielding)

Words from foreign languages

(1) A   (3) C   (5) A   (7) A
(2) D   (4) B   (6) A   (8) C

(9) D	(20) B	(31) D	(42) C
(10) C	(21) A	(32) A	(43) B
(11) B	(22) B	(33) D	(44) B
(12) A	(23) C	(34) B	(45) D
(13) B	(24) B	(35) A	(46) A
(14) D	(25) D	(36) C	(47) B
(15) B	(26) B	(37) C	(48) A
(16) C	(27) A	(38) B	(49) C
(17) A	(28) D	(39) C	(50) C
(18) B	(29) B	(40) D	
(19) D	(30) C	(41) A	

Words similar in form but different in meaning

(1) A4 B1	(14) A3 B1	(27) A2 B4	(40) A5 B4
(2) A1 B3	(15) A1 B4	(28) A5 B2	(41) A3 B2
(3) A2 B5	(16) A4 B5	(29) A5 B4	(42) A5 B4
(4) A5 B2	(17) A3 B1	(30) A5 B2	(43) A3 B1
(5) A4 B2	(18) A1 B5	(31) A4 B3	(44) A4 B2
(6) A2 B3	(19) A1 B3	(32) A5 B4	(45) A5 B2
(7) A5 B2	(20) A3 B5	(33) A1 B3	(46) A2 B4
(8) A2 B3	(21) A1 B4	(34) A3 B2	(47) A3 B2
(9) A1 B4	(22) A4 B3	(35) A1 B4	(48) A5 B1
(10) A4 B1	(23) A4 B2	(36) A3 B2	(49) A4 B2
(11) A2 B3	(24) A2 B5	(37) A4 B5	(50) A5 B3
(12) A4 B2	(25) A1 B3	(38) A1 B5	
(13) A3 B2	(26) A5 B2	(39) A5 B2	

Words with more than one meaning

(1) rest	(18) quarry	(35) coast
(2) sound	(19) tender	(36) pet
(3) bank	(20) frank	(37) mould
(4) stern	(21) saw	(38) invalid
(5) present	(22) graze	(39) see
(6) draw	(23) flounder	(40) pale
(7) fine	(24) utter	(41) spray
(8) van	(25) purse	(42) gloss
(9) close	(26) jar	(43) stole
(10) grave	(27) rifle	(44) spoils
(11) grate	(28) fence	(45) hack

(12) smack
(13) court
(14) bluff
(15) barracks
(16) rush
(17) shock

(29) relief
(30) flag
(31) brood
(32) tumbler
(33) strain
(34) leaves

(46) retort
(47) object
(48) continent
(49) entrance
(50) impregnable

Homophones

(1) A. dye
B. die

(2) A. road
B. rode

(3) A. peace
B. piece

(4) A. vain
B. vein

(5) A. rough
B. ruff

(6) A. whine
B. wine

(7) A. bough
B. bow

(8) A. sighs
B. size

(9) A. stile
B. style

(10) A. fair
B. fare

(11) A. slay
B. sleigh

(12) A. beer
B. bier

(13) A. bass
B. base

(18) A. knave
B. nave

(19) A. plain
B. plane

(20) A. peak
B. pique

(21) A. guessed
B. guest

(22) A. allowed
B. aloud

(23) A. pried
B. pride

(24) A. cygnet
B. signet

(25) A. cymbal
B. symbol

(26) A. chaste
B. chased

(27) A. sight
B. cite

(28) A. bard
B. barred

(29) A. bolder
B. boulder

(30) A. braid
B. brayed

(35) A. choler
B. collar

(36) A. populous
B. populace

(37) A. adds
B. adze

(38) A. invade
B. inveighed

(39) A. gamble
B. gambol

(40) A. raise
B. raze

(41) A. grisly
B. grizzly

(42) A. faint
B. feint

(43) A. discreet
B. discrete

(44) A. levee
B. levy

(45) A. auger
B. augur

(46) A. canvas
B. canvass

(47) A. rheum
B. room

119

(14) A. caught B. court	(31) A. brews B. bruise	(48) A. gin B. Jinn
(15) A. profit B. prophet	(32) A. weather B. wether	(49) A. fawn B. faun
(16) A. taught B. taut	(33) A. hoar B. whore	(50) A. tocsin B. toxin
(17) A. holy B. wholly	(34) A. moat B. mote	

Synonyms

(1) slay	(18) vaunt	(35) fallacious
(2) rage	(19) brawl	(36) douse
(3) love	(20) abhor	(37) aver
(4) loud	(21) warm	(38) spurious
(5) face	(22) reek	(39) equine
(6) threat	(23) inter	(40) puma
(7) plot	(24) strew	(41) urbane
(8) release	(25) yearn	(42) vitiate
(9) remain	(26) précis	(43) inveigh
(10) evade	(27) revile	(44) indict
(11) pledge	(28) verve	(45) ghost
(12) stalk	(29) abyss	(46) hone
(13) greet	(30) lewd	(47) cursory
(14) laud	(31) relish	(48) fecund
(15) revolve	(32) rime	(49) otiose
(16) vault	(33) immerse	(50) deliquesce
(17) flay	(34) naive	

Tests of usage and verbal reasoning

Transposition of words

(1) mistakes/people	(21) ways/error
(2) goalkeeper/crossbar	(22) time/motion
(3) man/strength	(23) confined/trapped
(4) serious/developed	(24) cause/conscience
(5) house/end	(25) if/when
(6) valour/discretion	(26) he/nobody

(7) recent/confusing
(8) comfort/four
(9) met/accepted
(10) eruption/ash
(11) passengers/pilot
(12) countryside/forest
(13) anticipated/paid
(14) rain/sunshine
(15) interest/places
(16) like/say
(17) total/growing
(18) every/very
(19) critics/performers
(20) adversity/community
(27) professional/amateur
(28) resources/encouragement
(29) right/move
(30) stability/employment
(31) great/modest
(32) you/are
(33) danger/presence
(34) will/can
(35) examples/archaeologists
(36) little/any
(37) about/of
(38) issues/differences
(39) Spain/bullfighting
(40) its/it's

The right word in the right place

(1) C	(11) B	(21) B	(31) A
(2) A	(12) C	(22) D	(32) B
(3) B	(13) B	(23) C	(33) D
(4) A	(14) C	(24) A	(34) B
(5) D	(15) C	(25) D	(35) B
(6) B	(16) B	(26) A	(36) C
(7) A	(17) A	(27) B	(37) C
(8) C	(18) B	(28) A	(38) D
(9) B	(19) A	(29) D	(39) B
(10) D	(20) D	(30) B	(40) A

Relationships between words

(1) 3 A	(11) 3 D	(21) 3 B	(31) 1 C
(2) 2 B	(12) 1 B	(22) 2 A	(32) 3 B
(3) 1 C	(13) 2 C	(23) 4 C	(33) 2 C
(4) 1 B	(14) 4 C	(24) 2 C	(34) 1 B
(5) 3 A	(15) 2 D	(25) 2 A	(35) 4 A
(6) 2 D	(16) 3 C	(26) 3 B	(36) 1 D
(7) 3 B	(17) 1 C	(27) 2 A	(37) 3 C
(8) 4 B	(18) 2 A	(28) 4 D	(38) 4 B
(9) 2 D	(19) 3 C	(29) 3 A	(39) 2 A
(10) 2 A	(20) 4 A	(30) 2 B	(40) 2 C

Odd ones out

(1) B F	(11) A D	(21) B C	(31) C E
(2) C F	(12) A E	(22) D F	(32) C F
(3) A B	(13) C D	(23) A D	(33) C E
(4) C E	(14) B D	(24) A B	(34) B F
(5) B D	(15) A F	(25) A C	(35) C F
(6) D F	(16) B F	(26) A F	(36) A C
(7) C E	(17) D F	(27) A B	(37) C D
(8) A E	(18) B C	(28) C E	(38) B F
(9) C F	(19) A F	(29) A F	(39) D F
(10) D F	(20) E F	(30) B D	(40) A F

Further Reading from Kogan Page

The Business Guide to Effective Speaking, Jacqueline Dunckel and Elizabeth Parnham
The Business Guide to Effective Writing, J A Fletcher and D F Gowing
The Business Writing Workbook, Ian Stewart
How to Study: A Student's Guide to Effective Learning Skills, Anne Howe
Improving Your Presentation Skills, Michael Stevens
A Practical Guide to Effective Listening, Diane Bone
Readymade Business Letters, Jim Dening
Speak with Confidence, Meribeth Bunch

Better Management Skills

Creative Thinking in Business, Carol Kinsey Goman
Effective Meeting Skills: How to Make Meetings More Productive, Marion E Haynes
Effective Performance Appraisals, Robert B Maddux
Effective Presentation Skills, Steve Mandel
How to Communicate Effectively, Bert Decker
How to Develop a Positive Attitude, Elwood N Chapman
Make Every Minute Count: How to Manage Your Time Effectively, Marion E Haynes
Successful Negotiation, Robert B Maddux